The Boston RED SOX

Howard Liss
Editor of Baseball Series: Gene Schoor

Simon and Schuster
NEW YORK

Copyright © 1982 by Gene Schoor
All rights reserved
including the right of reproduction
in whole or in part in any form
Published by Simon and Schuster
A Division of Gulf & Western Corporation
Simon & Schuster Building
Rockefeller Center
1230 Avenue of the Americas
New York, New York 10020

SIMON AND SCHUSTER and colophon are
trademarks of Simon & Schuster
Designed by Irving Perkins Associates
Manufactured in the United States of America

1 2 3 4 5 6 7 8 9 10

Library of Congress Cataloging in Publication Data

Liss, Howard.
The Boston Red Sox.

1. Boston Red Sox (Baseball team)—History.
I. Title.
GV875.B62L56   796.357'64'0974461   82-676
AACR2

ISBN 0-671-42058-5

Acknowledgments

The author wishes to acknowledge a debt of gratitude to all those who helped him with this exciting project.

To the entire staff of the Boston Red Sox and especially to VP Haywood Sullivan, Buddy LeRoux, public relations director Bill Crowley and his chief aide, Jack McCarthy;

to Seymour Cohen, sports commentator on radio station WATD in Boston;

to the Red Sox photography department and to Wide World Photos for the numerous photos;

to my great editor at Simon and Schuster, Peter Schwed, and to my agent, Julian Bach, who aided and encouraged me;

and a special debt to the late Fred Lieb, newspaperman, sports editor and columnist, for his wonderful stories on the Red Sox through the years;

Finally, to the Fenway faithful . . . who wait . . . wait . . . till next year. . . .

*For Seymour and Lynn Cohen of Duxbury . . .
two fantastic Red Sox boosters*

Chapter I

BASEBALL WAS a Boston tradition long before the Red Sox were born. Contrary to the popular legend that had Abner Doubleday inventing it in 1839, different forms of the game were being played during the latter part of the eighteenth century. Among them were "One Old Cat," "Town Ball" and "New York Ball," all stemming from variations of two English games, cricket and rounders. Rounders was played on the Boston Common early in the nineteenth century, and Dr. Oliver Wendell Holmes (the noted physician and father of Supreme Court Justice Holmes) recalled having enjoyed the game while at Harvard, from which he graduated in 1829.

Essentially, rounders was a loose game in which runners were put out by "soaking"—hitting them with a thrown ball—and a team had to score one hundred runs in order to win. The Boston Game, as it was then called, reached the height of its popularity in 1857, for by then such teams as the Boston Olympics, the Elm Trees and the Green Mountains had been formed and were playing on the Common. Business came to a standstill on Saturday afternoons as spectators gathered to watch. So popular was the sport that it spread to village greens throughout New England. But soon a menace loomed on the horizon, and the Boston Game was doomed to die out. The threat came from New York.

A different version of baseball was being played in the New York area. The ball was bigger and the infield was a diamond, whereas Boston's was a box. In 1857 a watch-case maker named Edward G. Satzman, who had played in New York for a team called the Gothams, moved to Boston, and he taught his game to his co-workers. Eventually, he formed the Tri-Mountains, a team which played by New York rules. Since New Yorkers streamed into the area, particularly to such institutions of learning as Harvard, Andover and Exeter, their impact on baseball was enormous. When the New York Game was played on the Common, the Boston Game was about finished.

Albert Spalding, one of baseball's first great stars, has been quoted as saying, "Just as Boston was the cradle of liberty, so was it the cradle in which the infant game was helped to a healthy maturity." History bears him out. The first intercollegiate baseball game was played between Amherst and Williams in 1859 (won by Amherst, 73–33) in Pittsfield. Furthermore, the first Harvard Book of Athletics (published in 1924) claims that not only did the Harvard and Lowell clubs draw the first crowd that reached five figures (on the Common in 1865), but, in addition, three elements of the game were invented at Harvard: the original catcher's mask, which is still on display at Briggs Cage in Cambridge, the pitcher's change of pace, and the spitball.

The cause of Boston baseball was furthered by the overwhelming success of America's first professional baseball team, the Cincinnati Red Stockings, or Reds. The Reds went through the entire 1869 season undefeated, and were not beaten until June 14th, 1870, when the Brooklyn Atlantics ended their sixty-five-game winning streak. Before that, the touring Reds had visited the Boston area and defeated such teams as the Lowells, Harvards and Tri-Mountains by big scores. A Boston businessman named Ivers Whitney Adams wanted a team like that for his city, and on January 20th, 1871, the wheels were set in motion.

Adams had his eye on the two mainstays of the Reds, Harry and George Wright. They were the sons of a noted English cricket player, and had learned to play the British game before being introduced to the mysteries of baseball. Harry was the center fielder and captain of the Reds and was paid twelve hundred dollars a year. Brother George was the shortstop, and his salary was fourteen hundred dollars. Ivers Whitney Adams figured, not unreasonably, that these two men could put Boston on the baseball map, but he also realized that there had to be some kind of league to bind a group of teams together. From that gathering came an organization called the National Association of Professional Base Ball Players. The teams involved came from Boston, New York, Chicago, Philadelphia, Washington, Brooklyn, Fort Wayne, Cleveland and Rockford, Illinois. Oddly, Cincinnati, which had done so much for baseball, was not included.

However, certain elements of the Cincinnati club were acquired by Boston. There were the Wright brothers, catcher-outfielder Cal McVey and first baseman Charley Gould, who formed the core of the new team. Also adopted were the red hose which had served Cincinnati so well. The Boston team became known as the Red Stockings.

Spring training for the 1871 season was conducted indoors at the Tremont Gymnasium, and on April 6th the team played its first game at the South End Grounds. All things considered, the Boston team did quite well in its initial season, finishing second to Philadelphia. For the next four years it was all Boston.

From 1872 through 1875, the Red Stockings reigned supreme. That they finished first constantly was beside the point; it was merely that they practically ran away and hid from the rest of the league, rolling up percentages of .830, .729, .717 and finally an unbelievable .899 in 1875, when the team won seventy-one and lost only eight, including twenty-six victories in a row and all thirty-eight home games. Overall, the Red Stockings racked up a 205–50 record, which will probably never be approached, let alone equaled.

In 1874 the Red Stockings and the Philadelphia club traveled to England in order to introduce Britishers to their game. The tour itself was far from successful. English sportsmen had no idea what baseball was all about and showed their lack of enthusiasm by staying away en masse. So, just to prove a point, the Red Stockings formed a cricket team, starring three Wright brothers (Sam Wright accompanied the tour), Cap Anson, Al Reach and a few others. They took on Britain's vaunted Marylebone cricket team and beat them handily. The athletic talent of these men was indisputable. Reach, Wright and Albert Spalding, the Red Stockings' star pitcher, later became famous as manufacturers of sporting goods equipment.

After the 1875 season, William A. Hulbert of Chicago decided he'd had enough of Boston's domination. Secretly, he made a deal for Spalding to jump to his White Sox, and then Hulbert added Cal McVey, Cap Anson, Ross Barnes and Deacon Jim White, the core of the Boston team.

Not until late in the year did the news leak out, after a Chicago paper broke the story. The Civil War had ended a scant ten years earlier, which explained why the lads of Boston considered the players who jumped the Red Stockings guilty of treason. "You dirty seceders, your white stockings will be soiled," they shouted as the offending players walked the Boston streets.

The actions of these players, and others who jumped their teams later, helped bring about the "reserve clause" in 1879, a rule which bound a player to the team that originally signed him, until he was sold, traded, released or retired. The reserve clause remained in effect for almost a century, until arbitrator Peter Seitz overruled it in January 1976, in the Andy Messersmith-Dave McNally cases.

Hulbert did more than raid the Red Stockings. The National Association was not on firm financial ground, and Hulbert thought baseball should be run as a business. He told Albert Spalding, "I've got a new scheme. Let us anticipate those eastern cusses and organize an association of our own. Then we'll see who does the expelling."

In February 1876, during a meeting of all interested teams at New York's Broadway Central Hotel, Hulbert proposed a new grouping, to be called the National *League* of Professional Base Ball Clubs. Thus was the National League formed, and the National Association collapsed. Initially, Hulbert's organization consisted of Chicago, St. Louis, Cincinnati and Louisville in the Midwest, and New York, Philadelphia, Boston and Hartford in the East. Along the way, for various reasons, some of the teams were dropped, but the new league continued to play ball.

Hulbert's White Sox won the pennant in 1876, but Harry Wright was not idle. He gathered some good players, including Deacon Jim White, who returned to the Red Stockings in 1877, and then Boston was back as the champ. Then, with great players such as outfielders Hugh Duffy and Tommy McCarthy, they racked up pennants in 1891, 1892, 1893, 1897 and 1898. Strangely, as time went by, the name Red Stockings seemed dated, and by the turn of the century the club was known as the Beaneaters.

The arrogance of the National League angered a number of independent baseball-team owners. In the winter of 1881, a sportswriter named Albert Spink spearheaded a drive to form another major league, called the American Association. Among the teams were clubs from Brooklyn, Pittsburgh, Philadelphia, Cincinnati, St. Louis and Louisville, the last later replaced by Baltimore. While the American Association used many National League rules, it also differed somewhat, in that games were played on Sundays and holidays, the sale of beer was allowed, and admission was twenty-five cents, half the price of a National League ticket.

The competition between the two leagues helped drive up salaries and caused teams to raid each other's rosters. In time, however, peace was made, with all teams agreeing to respect each other's territorial rights and player contracts. But new difficulties continued to arise through the 1890s as the greed of the owners and the stupidity of the players manifested itself in numerous ways.

The owners cheated the players—and each other—mercilessly. Gate receipts were often falsely reported, so that visiting teams did not get their fair share. With total control over their players, owners could—and did—cut salaries with impunity, sometimes as much as forty percent. Players were fined for the slightest reason, paychecks were withheld, reasonable expenses were not paid.

The attitude of the players was little better. Often a ball game would degenerate into a brawl because players used any means, fair or foul, to win. Umpires had little authority and were abused and shoved around. The owners paid no attention to what was going on because they were interested in gate receipts and nothing else. The National League was in danger of disintegrating under the weight of its own grossness.

There were, however, some knowledgeable baseball men who were bent on changing things for the better. One was Charles Comiskey, manager of the Cincinnati club; another was a keen, intelligent sportswriter for the *Cincinnati Gazette* named Bancroft Johnson. They understood that the game had to be cleaned up if only for the benefit of the fans, who were becoming disenchanted with the avarice of baseball's personnel. The National League seemingly wasn't interested in reform, so these two men, and others, took matters into their own hands.

In 1894 the Western League was formed. It was a minor league composed of midwestern cities, but perhaps even then plans were afoot for a confrontation with the entrenched National League. Certainly the men involved seemed to have ideas in that direction, but prudently they bided their time.

Comiskey was awarded the St. Paul franchise, and Milwaukee went to a tall, skinny ex-catcher named Cornelius McGillicuddy, later known as Connie Mack, one of baseball's true immortals. Ban Johnson was nominated as president of the new organization, a position he promptly accepted.

Everything began to jell for baseball's revival in 1899, when Ban Johnson announced the reorganization of his Western Association and declared that his group would begin playing in 1900 as the American League. It was not his intention to start another baseball war, he said, but simply to fulfill the urgent need to give the game a new look. Johnson began implementing his ideas immediately.

Umpires were given proper authority to conduct games in an orderly manner. Drinking, gambling, profanity and all rowdyism were absolutely prohibited; those who failed to abide by Johnson's rules were fined or suspended. Fans warmed to this brand of sports and showed their approval by supporting the new league with satisfying attendance numbers. The new league began to make money.

The National League was in no mood for peaceful coexistence. Already splitting apart with internal dissension, the moguls decided to regroup. Four of the twelve teams were dropped: Cleveland, Louisville, Washington and Baltimore. Johnson moved a team into Cleveland and also placed Comiskey in Chicago, and then declared that the American League was the second major league in the land. Connie Mack, without much financial backing, moved into Philadelphia, to be replaced in Milwaukee by Hugh Duffy from the Boston Beaneaters.

And then, as though defying the National League to stop him, Johnson announced new teams in Washington and Boston.

The National League powers thought Johnson was only bluffing. A lot of money was required to establish new franchises, and some NL owners predicted the speedy demise of this ambitious plan. Besides, where would the players come from? Brooklyn's Charles Ebbets said, "When the time comes for advance money, they will all weaken. The demands of these players are preposterous."

But Ban Johnson did have a financial backer in the person of Charles Somers, a coal, lumber and shipping magnate. Somers financed Cleveland and loaned money to Connie Mack, and made an additional loan of ten thousand dollars to Comiskey. Somers then convinced Ben Shibe, who manufactured Reach baseballs, to take over in Philadelphia while he handled Boston. Since Somers had a piece of four teams, the first six American League pennants were won by his teams. Today, of course, such a monopoly would be completely illegal.

After casting about for the site of a new playing field, a lease was signed on a stretch of land on Huntington Avenue, not far from Roxbury. Once it had been the site of touring carnivals and Buffalo Bill's Wild West shows, a good-sized area of approximately 287,000 square feet. The land was owned by the New York, New Haven and Hartford Railroad, and the Boston Elevated Railway had a lease on it. When a check signed by Charles Somers was handed to the railway company, the agent seemed somewhat skeptical. He asked his bank to contact Somers's Cleveland bank, and received this reply: "Draw on us to the extent of $100,000." That was quite a bit of money at the turn of the twentieth century.

If Boston had any doubts about the seriousness of the new franchise, their fears were immediately dispelled when Jimmy Collins was signed as manager. Collins, recognized as the greatest of all third basemen, had been playing for the National League team in Boston, but he couldn't squeeze any money out of them, despite the fact that he was a key man on the team. He was the first third baseman to charge in and field bunts with the sureness of a master. Collins was only five feet seven and weighed 160 pounds, but he hit with surprising power. Jimmy usually hit well over .300, and though he fell below that average in his later years, he did post a fourteen-year average of .296.

At a press conference, Collins explained why he jumped to the new league: "I like to play baseball, but this is a business with me, and I can't be governed by sentiment. Repeatedly in the past I asked [the NL franchise boss] for a salary increase, but I was put aside with one flimsy excuse or another. Only this winter, with the American League in the field, have they shown any sign of granting it."

Collins was paid either four thousand or five thousand dollars for the season, depending on whom the fans listened to. However, the Boston National team failed to listen to anyone, for Collins was able to steal from their ranks such fine players as center fielder Chick Stahl, right fielder Buck Freeman and pitcher Ted Lewis. Stahl later became manager of the new Boston team.

Freeman was a fine hitter. Despite his comparatively small stature—five feet nine inches, 155 pounds—he hit the unheard-of total of twenty-five home runs for the Washington National League team in 1899. After joining the new team he averaged 113 runs-batted-in per season from 1901 to 1903, leading the league in 1902 and '03. Ted Lewis later coached at Harvard, became president of Massachusetts State College and was president of the University of New Hampshire at the time of his death in 1936. Collins got a couple of additional players from the Boston Nationals the following year, causing Frank Selee, their manager, to leave town.

However, Collins's greatest coup came when Frank Robison, who owned both the Cleveland Spiders and St. Louis

Nationals, tried to transfer his magnificent battery of Cy Young and Lou Criger from Cleveland to St. Louis. Young refused to make the move, enabling Collins to steal the pitcher, the catcher and another pitcher named George Cuppy.

Denton Tecumseh Young, a farm boy from Gilmore, Ohio (his real middle name was True), earned the nickname Cy because any hick fresh from the farm was called "Cy" or "Cyrus" in those days. And if anyone in the United States ever looked like a rube from the sticks, it was Young. When he joined the Spiders, after pitching a minor-league no-hit game for Canton, Ohio, against McKeesport of the Tri-State League, in which he recorded eighteen strikeouts, he wore a low-crowned derby hat, and that was too small for his head. Furthermore, six inches of wrist and ankle stuck out of his jacket and pants. Davis Hawley, secretary-treasurer of the Spiders, almost fainted when he saw him. Hawley said that Young looked just like a scarecrow in the field. Fearing that the entire Spiders team would collapse with laughter when they saw him, Hawley rushed him to a clothing store and bought him a complete new outfit before introducing him at the clubhouse.

In his first NL game against Chicago, Young beat Cap Anson's team, allowing just three hits. After the game Hawley and Anson had a friendly chat, during which Anson remarked, "That big rube had a lot of luck beating us today. He's too green to do your club much good, but I believe I could make a pitcher out of him in a couple of years. Anyway, I'm willing to give you a thousand dollars for him."

Hawley lit his cigar and grinned. "If I recall correctly, that big rube struck you out twice, Cap, and I think he can do it again. I'm sure he can do us as much good as he would Chicago, so you keep your thousand and we'll keep the rube."

In his first big-league season, Young won twenty-seven games, and that was the start of a career which saw him win an incredible total of 511 games, a record that will probably endure forever. (A pitcher winning twenty-five games per year for twenty years would still fall short of Young's number.)

When Collins obtained Young, the six-feet two-inch, 210-pound farmboy was already thirty-four years old, and he got off to a poor start, but he soon got himself together and was 33–10 at the end of the year, leading the new league in wins, in earned-run average (1.62), strikeouts (158), fewest walks per nine innings (0.90), fewest hits per nine innings (7.85) and most shutouts (five). He was second in winning percentage, complete games, innings and games pitched.

As backups for Criger, Collins acquired two free spirits named Ossee Schreckengost and Larry (real name John) McLean. Schreck lasted only one year with Boston and betook himself to Philadelphia where he buddied up with a pitcher named Rube Waddell, and together they drove both the opposition and Connie Mack to despair. Once the pair got themselves thrown out of a swank New Orleans hostelry for nailing a steak to the dining room wall. They were so close that they shared the same double bed on road trips, which led to clauses in both contracts that might well defy the talents of modern attorneys. Schreck demanded a clause in Waddell's contract prohibiting him from eating crackers in bed, while Waddell held out for a clause in Schreck's contract banning the eating of "pizzazza sandwiches" in bed, since Schreck's snack contained liberal doses of limburger cheese and onions.

While the Huntington Avenue grounds were being prepared, Boston opened the season in Baltimore on April 26th, 1901, with the following lineup:

Tommy Dowd, lf; Charles Hemphill, rf; Chick Stahl, cf; Jimmy Collins, 3b; Buck Freeman, 1b; Freddy Parent, ss; Hobe Ferris, 2b; Lou Criger, c; Winford Kellum, p.

The first three road games were a disaster for the Boston Americans. Kellum lost, 10–6, then Cy Young was bombed and didn't make it through the third inning, as Baltimore won, 17–6. One newspaper was especially rough on Young. The article declared, "Who said Young is so good? The farmer is thirty-four, and probably left his fast pitch in Cleveland."

Now Boston journeyed to Philadelphia and was beaten again as George Cuppy took the loss, 8–6. Not until game four, also against the Athletics, did Boston break into the win column, as Young pitched a shaky 8–6 victory. Then the club took on Washington and Baltimore again, losing four out of the five games.

"We're too anxious," Collins remarked. "We're trying too hard and beating ourselves . . . but we are going to show better pitching in the near future."

Probably the contractors on the Huntington Avenue site knew they were part of history in the making, for the field was ready when the club returned home. The sod was in place, with a little grandstand seating 2,600 and bleachers holding another 6,500 already erected. There was also ample standing room behind ropes in left and right field.

On May 8th, 1901, the future of Boston baseball was evident to anyone who cared to look. On one side of the tracks the Boston Americans played Philadelphia, while on the other side the Boston Nationals took on the 1900 champion Brooklyn team. Jimmy Collins and his crew drew 11,500 fans, a total sellout, while the Nationals drew 5,500. However, many of the NL "fans" were students from Boston English and Latin High School, who came in on free passes, so that the paying crowd was closer to three thousand. Both Boston teams won, but it was clear that Boston belonged to the American League. Less than fifty-one years later, the National League team, then known as the Braves, moved to Milwaukee and then to Atlanta. The National League had dug its own grave in the Land of the Bean and the Cod.

Chapter II

FOR ITS first Saturday game with Baltimore, Boston drew eight thousand fans, and it was then that Ban Johnson made his presence felt as president of the new league. Boston lost, 8–7, despite a five-run rally in the ninth inning. During that rally, scrappy John McGraw of the Orioles got somewhat testy with the umpires, with the result that he was suspended for five games. Johnson thus served notice that he would not permit his umpires to be treated the way the umpires were handled in the National League.

Boston finished in second place in its maiden season, four games behind the champion White Sox. Many of the players had outstanding years; Young, of course, became the idol of Boston with his thirty-one wins, and other pitchers who contributed handsomely were George Winters, who was fresh from Gettysburg College and won sixteen, a total matched by Parson Lewis. The batting hero was Buck Freeman, whose .346 average was second only to Nap Lajoie of the Athletics, who raked enemy pitchers with a .405 average. Freeman's mark included twelve home runs, twenty-two doubles, fifteen triples and 114 RBIs. Other stalwarts included Collins at .329, Ossee Schreck with .320, Fred Parent at .318 and Chick Stahl who batted .310. The team average was .293, which was remarkable in the era of the dead ball.

With 527,548 paid admissions (only eighteen thousand less than the champion White Sox), the Boston Americans outdrew their National League rivals by about 200,000 fans. One problem that the Boston Americans failed to solve during those early years was the lack of a name.

Generally, they were referred to as "the Bostons," which meant absolutely nothing. Hometown newspapers referred to the club by any number of names, including "the Pilgrims," "the Puritans" and "the Plymouth Rocks," but none of them caught on. On the road some sportswriters called the team "the Somersets," perhaps indicating their debt to Charles Somers, or perhaps thinking of the Somerset Hotel. Not until 1907 was the name "Red Sox" used.

In 1902 Collins added a few more players, and in one instance a deal was made which could not possibly happen today. It involved a first baseman named George "Candy" LaChance, a big, likeable French Canadian from Putnam, Connecticut, who had played for Cleveland the previous season. At the time Somers owned Cleveland as well as Boston, and still retained an interest in Philadelphia. Therefore, he sent LaChance to Boston and brought Ossee Schreck to Philadelphia. Other players new to the Boston Americans included Bill Dineen, a standout pitcher who jumped the Beaneaters. Dineen, a native of Syracuse, New York, quickly joined Cy Young as one of the great pitchers of the early Red Sox staff. Dineen won twenty-one games that first year, came back to win twenty-one in 1903, twenty-three in 1904 and then dropped off, winning fourteen in 1905. After a marvelous twelve-year career, Dineen served as one of the American League's outstanding umpires. Other players new to Boston in 1902 included the New York Giants battery of pitcher Frank Sparks and catcher Jack Warner, outfielder Pat Dougherty and pitcher Tom Hughes.

"Screwy baseball," was the phrase Collins used to describe the 1902 season. The team played .600 ball against first-division teams and only .532 against the second four clubs. Boston finished third, six and a half games behind the winning Athletics, and again the Somers touch was in evidence.

Connie Mack had raided the Phillies, acquiring some outstanding players, including Nap Lajoie, but the Pennsylvania Supreme Court upheld the legality of the reserve clause and ordered the players back. Two pitchers did obey and return, but three others moved on to Cleveland where the Pennsylvania court could not touch them. Mack was desperate for pitchers, so Somers let him have three of his own. In mid-June, Mack captured Rube Waddell from Los Angeles and also Danny Murphy. Waddell went on to win twenty-three games for Mack after June 26th.

In that era of pitching immortals, some of the greatest duels in baseball annals saw Waddell matched up against Cy Young. For example, on May 5th, 1904, Young bested Waddell by pitching a perfect game. The following season Waddell beat Young, 3–2, in a cliffhanger that lasted twenty innings. It should be added that the National League had its own version of champ-against-champ, with Mordecai "Three-Finger" Brown of the Cubs going head-to-head against Christy Mathewson of the Giants. In 1905 Brown and Mathewson pitched no-hitters against each other for nine innings, but finally Brown allowed a pair of hits and the Giants won, 1–0. Then Brown beat Mathewson nine straight times.

Peace came to baseball in January 1903, when the National League was forced to concede that the American League upstarts were indeed a major league. Under the treaty, the National League allowed the Americans to shift a franchise from Baltimore to New York City, provided they also agreed to stay out of Pittsburgh. Also, the disposition of fifteen players was settled, and Ban Johnson got the better of it. His league was awarded Ed Delahanty, Nap Lajoie, "Wee Willie" Keeler ("Hit 'em where they ain't"), Sam Crawford and Kid Elberfeld, while the Nationals got Christy Mathewson, Willis and Tommy Leach and a few lesser lights.

Charles Somers had been trying for two years to dispose of his interest in the Boston team, and he finally found someone in the person of Henry J. Killilea, a prominent Milwaukee attorney, who had been associated with Ban Johnson during the Western League days. Killilea brought in fellow Milwaukeean Joseph Smart as business manager, and the first item on the agenda was the ball park. It had been built on landfill and the winter snows with their resulting spring runoffs had turned the field into an excavation ditch. Workers were brought in and they toiled night and day to get the field ready for the home opening, which was to be on Patriots' Day. In spite of the peace, one more showdown had to take place between the two Boston baseball teams. Each had scheduled a morning-afternoon doubleheader, and both Philadelphia teams were in town as opponents. The holiday, which fell on Sunday that year, was celebrated on Monday, April 20th.

As far as the fans were concerned, it was really no contest.

True, the Athletics were the AL champions and Boston figured to outdraw their rivals, but the extent to which the fans went to show their favoritism was almost unbelievable. The American Leaguers drew 8,376 in the morning game while the Nationals drew 1,800. In the afternoon, 27,658 showed up at the Huntington Grounds while the Beaneaters drew 3,867 fans.

The Athletics pitched Waddell in the morning game, and it turned out to be one hilarious romp for Boston. Jimmy Collins knew that Waddell liked a few touches of booze at night and shunned an early bedtime like the plague. At ten in the morning a bleary-eyed Waddell took the mound and was greeted with a bunting attack that had him dizzy. He was chasing little taps along the foul lines until he was ready to drop, and looked pleadingly toward the dugout, hoping Mack would give him an early hook, but the skipper, ever the martinet, let his pitcher suffer.

"Get in there and pitch, you yellow so-and-so," screamed Athletics first baseman Harry Davis, while the hapless Waddell was running himself into the ground. Boston won, 9-4.

In the nightcap, Cy Young went against Eddie Plank, and Boston staked their pitcher to six runs. Plank was replaced by a young Indian named "Chief" Albert Bender, a muscular youth just nineteen years old. It was Bender's first major league appearance and he pitched superbly, holding Boston to just one run, a homer by Buck Freeman, while the Athletics jolted Young and his reliever, Tom Hughes, for ten runs.

Boston romped home easily in 1903, although the Athletics were still in the race as late as August 4th. Then Collins's men put on the pressure and steamed away. At the end of the season the Bostons were 103 percentage points ahead of Mack's team.

During the summer, it had become evident that Boston and Pittsburgh would win in their respective leagues, so the fans and sportswriters began a publicity campaign for a World Series between the two league champions. Both presidents, Killilea of Boston and Barney Dreyfuss of Pittsburgh, worked out an agreement which, to some extent at least, is still the basis for the modern Series.

One similarity lay in the roster, which is in use today. Both clubs agreed to use no player not under contract on September 1st (special dispensation is now required to replace an injured player). The differences lay in the number of games played and disbursement of money. At that time, the two clubs agreed to split gate receipts evenly and make their own financial arrangements with the players. It was to be a best-five-out-of-nine Series, with the first three games played in Boston, the next four in Pittsburgh, and the final two in Boston, should the Series go that far.

Pittsburgh had an outstanding pitching staff. In fact, the 1903 Pittsburgh staff holds the major-league record for successive shutouts, with six. Charles "Deacon" Phillippe had two and so did Sam Leever, while Irvin "Kaiser" Wilhelm and Ed Doheny had one each, in a streak that lasted from June 2nd through June 8th and covered fifty-six innings. Leever and Phillippe each won twenty-five games that year. Ed Doheny won sixteen, but the tall lefty went berserk right after the Series and had to be placed in an asylum.

For a time it seemed that the Series would never get under way. Boston players were under contract to play until September 30th, while Pittsburgh players had contracts lasting until October 30th. Boston players threatened to strike unless they received all of Boston's gate receipts. Killilea offered the players extra money, although he would keep the owner's share. Boston fans were taken aback at the idea of a strike. In the end the players agreed to Killilea's plan.

The Pirates stayed at the Vendome Hotel in Boston, and many fans came into the lobby to catch a glimpse of the National Leaguers. One fan spied Hans Wagner, the future Hall-of-Fame shortstop, and called out, "Hey, Dutchman, we're going to give you and the Pirates a good licking."

The easygoing Wagner shot back, "Who with—that old man Cy Young?"

It was a lively evening. Reportedly, some ten thousand dollars was bet on the outcome of the first game, and on the Series as well.

The opening-day crowd of 16,242 was packed along the foul lines and jammed against the outfield ropes. Cy Young took the mound against Deacon Phillippe, and the Bucs shelled the Boston ace for four runs in the first inning, going on to win, 7–3. Pittsburgh right fielder Jimmy Sebring had the honor of hitting the first home run in World Series history. Tommy Leach reached Young for a pair of triples, while Boston could manage only half a dozen hits off Phillippe. Boston played sloppy ball, with Ferris and Criger each committing two errors.

Bill Dineen evened the Series for Boston by tossing a 3–0 shutout, helped considerably by two home runs off the bat of Pat Dougherty. It was a tough game for Sam Leever to lose.

The third game was played on Saturday, October 3rd, before a crowd of 18,801, the largest of the entire Series. Fans spilled onto the playing field, making it difficult for the outfielders to run down fly balls, and the mixup in seats was enraging, as fans arrived bearing ticket stubs only to find the seats occupied. Fights broke out all over the ball park.

The Pirates won, 4–2, as Deacon Phillippe came back after only one day's rest to stop Boston on four hits—two by Jimmy Collins, who scored both Boston runs. The loser was Tom Hughes, who was knocked out in the third inning when the Pirates scored three runs. Cy Young relieved, but the damage was already done.

Pittsburgh got a break for game four. Sunday was a no-play date for both leagues, and rain washed out Monday's game, so that manager Fred Clarke was able to come back with his ace, Deacon Phillippe, who had all the time in the world to recuperate—two whole days! Collins countered with Dineen, but the Boston hurler didn't have it. In spite of the 150-man contingent of Boston fans called the Royal Rooters, who sang a song called "Tessie" at every opportunity, the Pirates won, 5–4. The Bucs banged Dineen for three runs in the seventh, highlighted by a pair of triples, and although Boston staged its own three-run rally in the ninth, it wasn't quite enough. The Pirates led in the Series, 3–1.

Boston was far from through. "Roaring Bill" Kennedy took on Collins's men while Cy Young took the responsibility for keeping Boston in the Series. For five innings the game was a scoreless tie, and then in the sixth the usually dependable Pittsburgh fielders fell apart. Errors by Wagner, Clarke and Leach opened the gates. Ten men batted and six scored. The Bostons added four more in the seventh and breezed in, 11–2. Even Young got in on the fun with a single and a triple.

Game six resulted in another Boston victory as Dineen beat Leever; the old schoolmaster was the victim of poor support as Leach made two errors and Wagner one. The final score was 6–3.

Pittsburgh owner Barney Dreyfuss tried to restore some order by having game seven postponed because of cold weather, but he had a double purpose in mind and the weather wasn't one of them. By waiting a day, Phillippe could pitch again. Also, by playing on Saturday instead of Friday, he could jampack 17,038 fans into Exposition Park, instead of the 10,200 he had averaged for the first three home games.

It was Phillippe against Young again, and the weather was still brisk and biting, but Young, the rube, did a lot better than his rival. Dreyfuss helped beat himself in a way.

Dreyfuss did get his overflow crowd, which cut down the area of the playing field. All balls hit into the crowd counted as ground-rule triples. Five of Boston's eleven hits were lofted into the crowd, most of them easy outs on a clear field. Young gave up only two ground-rule triples, and he was a rock with men on base, striking out six batters. Young beat Phillippe, 7–3, in a *must-win* game. Just to rub it in, Young and Dineen had held the great Hans Wagner hitless in eleven official times at bat.

Sunday was a day of rest, Monday was a rainy day, and Clarke threw Phillippe into the breach to halt Boston. Bill Dineen was ready to pitch. As he said later, "I want to get back to Syracuse. I got a lot of things I want to do. This thing has gone far enough."

Dineen closed the door on the 1903 World Series with a 3-0 shutout. He enjoyed perfect support in the field, especially one smart play by Lou Criger. With runners on first and third and two out, Wagner tried to steal second. Criger bluffed a throw to second, then whipped the ball to Collins at third, nailing Leach for the third out. The game ended as Wagner made the last out by fanning, and the delirious Boston fans streamed onto the field, singing, dancing and hollering, carrying their heroes to the dressing room.

Yet the Series left a sour taste with Boston fans, due to the machinations of Joe Smart, the business manager. Charges were leveled against Smart stating that he had been involved with ticket speculators, who reportedly had sold grandstand seats for five dollars each. Killilea's handling of gate receipts was also denounced. The Series drew 100,429 cash customers, producing a gate of $55,500. Dreyfuss threw his shares into the pot, so that each Pirate got a loser's share of $1,316. Killilea kept his owner's share of $6,699.65, so that each Boston player's share was less than the losers', amounting to $1,182, plus salary to October 15th.

Killilea's days as Boston's owner were numbered. The hostility of the press and the fans decreed a change in management, and shortly after the 1904 season got under way, Killilea was gone from the scene.

Chapter III

THE NEW owner of the Boston Pilgrims, as they were then called, was General Charles Henry Taylor, owner, publisher and editor of the *Boston Globe*. Taylor, a Civil War hero who had been gravely wounded in a battle at Port Hudson, Louisiana, in 1863, was one of Boston's great public-spirited citizens, having at one time been a clerk in the Massachusetts House of Representatives and also private secretary to Governor Claflin. General Taylor had little interest in owning a baseball team, but he purchased the team for his wild playboy son, John I. Taylor, with the idea that it would give him something to do and occupy his mind. General Taylor also had assured himself that the Boston Americans, World Champions of 1903, were a promising business venture. John F. "Honey Fitz" Fitzgerald, later mayor of Boston and grandfather of President John F. Kennedy, "Big Mike" Sullivan, and other important Boston politicians also had bids in for the ball club, but General Taylor closed the deal. Taylor's son, John I. Taylor, was a fine golfer, tennis player and polo star, but he loved baseball. He knew the game and had followed the Boston club avidly. He knew all the players and became president of the Boston team.

To his credit, John I. treated all newspapers, including the *Globe,* exactly the same, giving none of them a break over the others. However, he was a party to a trade that left the entire Boston community in an uproar, when he dealt the popular slugging outfielder Pat Dougherty to New York for an obscure utility infielder, Bob Unglaub. Until Harry Frazee ruined the

Red Sox in the post-World War I period, it was unquestionably the worst deal made by the Boston club.

To be fair, John I. was really doing a favor for Ban Johnson, who helped engineer the trade for the best of motives: Johnson wanted an American League team in New York City that could compete for fans with the New York Giants, a team skippered by the flamboyant John "Muggsy" McGraw. Besides, earlier in the season, Johnson had stuck his finger into another Boston-New York deal, which sent pitcher Tom Hughes and catcher Garland Stahl to the Highlanders in exchange for a good left-hander named Jesse Tannehill, who certainly pitched well for Boston. The Highlanders did improve—almost too much for Boston to handle.

Boston pitchers performed fabulous feats in 1904. Old Cy Young won twenty-six and lost sixteen, Bill Dineen posted a 23–14 record and Jesse Tannehill proved his worth by winning twenty-one and losing eleven. Some of the pitching duels they were involved in were nip and tuck, exciting ball down to the final out. For instance:

On May 1st, Rube Waddell pitched a one-hitter against Boston, beating Tannehill, 3–0. Only two Boston batters reached base. He then dared Young to face him, shouting, "I'll give you the same as I gave Tannehill."

On May 5th, Young called his bluff. Cyrus had his perfect game, setting down all twenty-seven Athletics in order, and again the score was 3–0. "How did you like that one, you hayseed?" Young shouted to the downcast Waddell.

Even Connie Mack had to admire Young's masterpiece. "I never saw such a game pitched," said the dignified Mack. "Cy was perfect! Just perfect!"

On August 15th, Jesse Tannehill also got into the act, hurling his own no-hitter, a game which saw only two White Sox get on base. However, Tannehill also came to grief that year. It was the era of spikes-high sliding, brush-back pitches and hard-nosed baseball, and Tannehill accidentally beaned Athletics outfielder Danny Hoffman, smashing the bone under his right eye. Hoffman almost died, and for weeks Tannehill was unable to throw an inside pitch to a batter, afraid of another beaning.

Young could be magnificent even in defeat. He hooked up with Eddie Plank of the Athletics in a duel that lasted thirteen innings. In one inning Danny Murphy cracked a triple off Young with nobody out. Up stepped Monte Cross, who took three swings and sat down. Mike Powers followed and he too struck out, swinging wildly before returning to the bench. Plank suffered the same fate. Nine pitched balls, nine swings, not one foul, not one called ball, just three outs. Young finally lost it, 1–0. The major leagues were alive with Hall-of-Fame pitchers then.

Of course, there were days when even the best pitchers were clobbered unmercifully. On one occasion the A's teed off on Young and Dineen, spraying base hits to all corners of the outfield. Chick Stahl, in center field, was running himself ragged chasing down line drives. Then a fan, paraphrasing Wee Willie Keeler, called out, "They're hittin' 'em where you ain't, Chick."

"Yeah," panted Stahl. "Why don't they hit 'em where I am for a change?"

The 1904 pennant race was a dandy. In the final days it boiled down to Boston and the New York Highlanders, with each taking turns leading, only to be caught and passed by the other. Finally, as was to happen so often in the future, the pennant hinged on a five-game series between the two teams. Boston went to Hilltop Park on 165th Street and Broadway in New York City, leading by half a game. It was the afternoon of Friday, October 7th.

Unfortunately, they ran into Jack Chesbro, a big-chested spitballer from North Adams, Massachusetts, who proceeded to win his record forty-first game, and by the evening of October 7th, with a 3–2 victory, the Highlanders led by half a game.

The following day's doubleheader in New York could not be played at the Highlander's home grounds because owner Frank Farrell had rented the field to Columbia University for a football game. The teams took the train to Boston for the Saturday doubleheader, knowing they were scheduled to return to New York for the Monday doubleheader that followed. Highlander manager Clark Griffith wanted Chesbro to remain behind so that he could be rested for the Monday fracas, but the big pitcher insisted on going.

"What the hell's the matter with me? Don't I work for this club anymore?" Chesbro demanded.

"But you worked yesterday," Griffith pointed out. "Do you want to pitch them all?"

"Don't you want to win the pennant?" Chesbro retorted.

Not only did Chesbro accompany the team to Boston, he also insisted on pitching the first game. Freddy Parent watched Chesbro warming up and muttered, "That fellow again? Doesn't he ever have enough?"

Chesbro should have remained at home. Boston fell upon him in the fourth for four runs, and continued the spree against Walter Clarkson. The final score was 13–2. Then Young and Jake Powell of the Highlanders dueled each other for seven innings until darkness fell. Boston won, 1–0. Powell allowed only four hits while New York combed Young for seven, but the fielding behind the old man was superb.

Boston now led by one and a half games with two left to play. A split would give them their second successive flag, but they had to get through a determined Chesbro in the first game. The big spitballer had had Sunday off and was primed to go in the first game of the twin bill.

The Highlanders took a 2–0 lead, one of the runs being driven in by their own Pat Dougherty, now wearing New York's uniform. But Chesbro's luck was still bad. With men on second and third, the second baseman threw wildly to the plate trying to get Candy LaChance, with the result that both runs scored. Then, in the ninth, one of Chesbro's spitters got away for a wild pitch and the winning run scored. There was no question that the ball had been thrown away. Years later, Kid Elberfeld told a sportswriter, "That was no passed ball. It was so far over the catcher's head, he couldn't have reached it standing on a stepladder."

John I. Taylor immediately challenged the New York Giants, winners in the National League, to another World Series, but New York owner John T. Brush wanted no part of a playoff. He disliked everyone connected with the American League—particularly the Highlanders, whom he called "the

Invaders." At one time, when the Highlanders were leading their league, New York sportswriters conjectured about the possible pitching matchups between Jack Chesbro and Christy Mathewson, or between "Iron Man" McGinnity and Jake Powell, and that didn't set well with Brush either.

Brush's players were anxious to play Boston, since it meant at least a thousand dollars or more per man, but manager John McGraw echoed the owner's sentiments. "They're just a bunch of bush leaguers," he said, dismissing Boston contemptuously. *The Sporting News* took a different view, calling the 1904 Boston club "World Champions by default."

That was the high point of John I. Taylor's ownership. Unexpectedly—almost overnight, it seemed—the team seemed to grow old. Boston skidded to fourth place as the big hitters slumped, bats fell silent as the Sox finished with a team batting average of .233. Cy Young won eighteen and lost nineteen, Bill Dineen won twelve and lost fifteen, and the infield of LaChance, Ferris, Parent and Collins was a step slower. An indicator of the team's slow collapse was the July 4th, 1905, doubleheader against the Athletics. After losing the opener, Boston sent Young to the mound while Mack countered with Waddell, and these incredible pitchers worked *twenty innings each* before Young finally lost, 4–2, on an error, a hit batter, two hits and a force play. Young gave up eighteen hits, Waddell only fifteen, and the Philly southpaw, after allowing two runs in the first inning, blanked Boston for the next nineteen.

The thirty-eight-year-old Young had near perfect control, which made the defeat all the more disheartening. "I'll be damned," he muttered. "I don't walk anybody in twenty innings and I still lose."

The following year Boston went down and out, ending up in the cellar, with a 49–105 record. A bitter feud developed between John I. and Jimmy Collins, with harsh words exchanged while the players looked and listened. Collins barred Taylor from the clubhouse, so Taylor placed a chair in the passageway to the clubhouse and berated the players as they left the field.

There were many reasons for Boston's collapse. Injuries plagued the team through 1906 with one regular or another being sidelined for varying periods. The encroachment of age didn't help, nor did the open dissension between owner and manager. Collins refused to put on his uniform after a while, which only inflamed the open wound between Taylor and the manager, and he finally turned his job over to Chick Stahl in August. Then began the parade of managers.

It started with tragedy. In the spring of 1907, Stahl, the player-manager, hurt his leg, and the doctors gave him a solution of carbolic acid and water for treatment. Stahl drank the solution and within the hour was dead. No one ever discovered why he did it. There seemed little explanation for the outfielder's rash act. Perhaps he brooded over the new material he was taking over, and the magnitude of his job frightened him. Chick had been married less than a year, and was apparently very happy. He was the offspring of German Catholic parents, and all through his career, no matter what demands baseball made upon him, he never forgot his religious duties. John I. Taylor was not at the training camp, and as far as it was known, Stahl had had no arguments with the chief in Boston, although it developed later that Stahl had tried to resign in Louisville three days before. It was a tragic training season for Boston fans.

Cy Young took over temporarily, making it plain he would serve only until a permanent manager could be found. The new man was George Huff, the former athletic director at the University of Illinois and a scout for the Chicago Cubs. Huff lasted exactly thirteen days. Evidently John I. didn't like the choice he'd made, and the second "permanent" manager was Bob Unglaub, who had come to Boston in the unpopular trade for Pat Dougherty. Unglaub was fired in mid-June and Jim McGuire, a forty-two-year-old catcher from New York, took charge. McGuire was fired in 1908 and replaced by Fred Lake, who was in turn replaced in 1910 by Patsy Donovan.

The old championship team of 1903 and '04 was dismantled. Candy LaChance was the first to go, followed in 1907 by Bill Dineen and Jimmy Collins and in 1908 by the second base combination of Ferris and Parent. That winter, Young and Criger were sent away. Yet, in spite of several bad deals, John I. did begin putting together a team that would come back by

1912. Over the lean years he brought in center fielder Tris Speaker and left fielder Duffy Lewis, pitchers Smokey Joe Wood and Eddie Cicotte, right fielder Harry Hooper and third baseman Larry Gardner.

Perhaps the departure of Cy Young was the most difficult of all for Boston fans to accept. The great pitcher's worth was demonstrated on June 8th, 1908, when he pitched his second no-hitter for Boston against the New York Americans. Players from around the league chipped in to buy him a loving cup, on which were engraved the words: FROM THE BALLPLAYERS OF THE AMERICAN LEAGUE TO SHOW THEIR APPRECIATION TO CY YOUNG AS A MAN AND AS A BALLPLAYER.

And, in 1907, John I. told the press that he would put red stockings on his team and call them the Red Sox. Then, in 1911, he and the old general authorized construction of a new ball park at the corner of Lansdowne and Jersey streets. Before the 1912 season, Taylor sold the team to Jim McAleer, manager of the Washington team, and Robert B. McRoy, Ban Johnson's aide and secretary of the American League. Jake Stahl, who also had an interest in the ownership of the team, returned to take over as first baseman-manager.

Regardless of John I. Taylor's temper tantrums, his constant changing of managers and his occasionally poor trades, the fans of Boston owe him a great debt. For it was this former playboy who gave the American League a team called the Red Sox and a new field named Fenway Park.

One of baseball's greatest pitchers, Cy Denton Young won more games than any other pitcher in baseball history. Cy won 511 games and lost 317 during a 22-year career that stretched from 1890 to 1911. Pitching for the Red Sox in 1901, Young won 33 games while losing 10. In 1903, Cy won 28 and lost 9, and won 2 games for the Bosox in the first World Series in baseball history, as the Red Sox defeated Pittsburgh 5 games to 3.

In 1901, the first Boston Americans posed for a team picture. Front row (left to right): Ossee Schreckengost, Lou Criger, Larry McLean, Jimmy Collins, pitcher Cy Young, Chick Stahl. Second row (partial identification): Fred Parent (second left), Hobe Ferris (fourth left), Buck Freeman (far right). Back row (left to right): Fred Mitchell, Harry Kane, Tom Dowd. Collins was the Americans' manager. The club finished in second place.

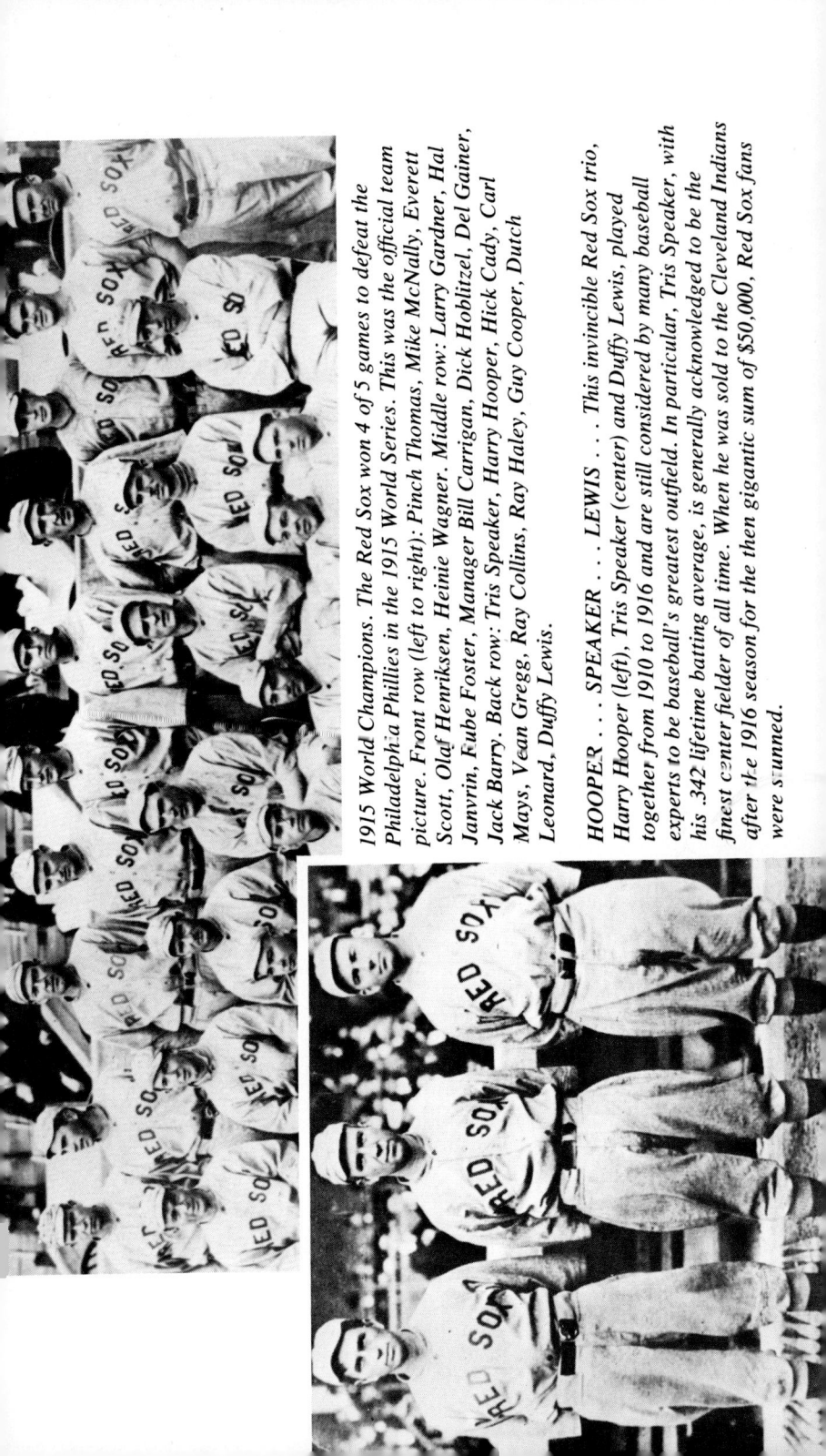

1915 World Champions. The Red Sox won 4 of 5 games to defeat the Philadelphia Phillies in the 1915 World Series. This was the official team picture. Front row (left to right): Pinch Thomas, Mike McNally, Everett Scott, Olaf Henriksen, Heinie Wagner. Middle row: Larry Gardner, Hal Janvrin, Rube Foster, Manager Bill Carrigan, Dick Hoblitzel, Del Gainer, Jack Barry. Back row: Tris Speaker, Harry Hooper, Hick Cady, Carl Mays, Vean Gregg, Ray Collins, Ray Haley, Guy Cooper, Dutch Leonard, Duffy Lewis.

HOOPER . . . SPEAKER . . . LEWIS . . . This invincible Red Sox trio, Harry Hooper (left), Tris Speaker (center) and Duffy Lewis, played together from 1910 to 1916 and are still considered by many baseball experts to be baseball's greatest outfield. In particular, Tris Speaker, with his .342 lifetime batting average, is generally acknowledged to be the finest center fielder of all time. When he was sold to the Cleveland Indians after the 1916 season for the then gigantic sum of $50,000, Red Sox fans were stunned.

THE BABE: *Babe Ruth, just 21 years old, pitching the Boston Red Sox to a 2–1 victory over the Brooklyn Dodgers in the 1916 World Series. The Babe was magnificent as he pitched the entire 14 innings, limiting the slugging Brooks to just 6 hits, while striking out 4. Del Gainer of the Red Sox won the game for the Bosox, when he doubled in the 14th to score McNally for the winning run. The Red Sox went on to win the World Series, 4 games to 1. Ruth, as a starting pitcher for the Red Sox from 1914-through 1919, won 89 games while losing but 46.*

Twenty-six years later, Babe Ruth at age 47 still shows his great pitching form. Here the Babe in his New York Yankees uniform takes to the mound in an exhibition game. The date, September 12, 1942.

Showing the effortless form that stamped him as perhaps baseball's greatest hitter, Ted Williams was "Teddy Ballgame" for the Red Sox from 1939 to 1960. A tremendous competitor, temperamental, a loner, a World War II and Korean fighter pilot, Williams will long be remembered along with DiMaggio, Ruth, Cobb, Speaker and Wagner as one of baseball's most colorful and greatest stars.

Dom DiMaggio was one of the finest center fielders in baseball from 1940 to 1951. He joined the Red Sox as a 22-year-old, promptly hit for a .301 average in his first year and was a fixture for 11 years. Here's Dom with brother Joe.

Friendly enemies . . . Ted Williams and Joe DiMaggio were bitter rivals during the 1940s and 1950s, when they were considered the two greatest stars in baseball. But they had great respect for each other's abilities. Joe always said, "Ted Williams is the greatest hitter I've ever seen." Williams would reply, "I think I can hit better than DiMaggio, but he really is the better all-around, most complete player."

During the 1940s and early '50s, this outstanding Red Sox infield, consisting of (left to right) Johnny Pesky, Vern Stephens, Bobby Doerr and Billy Goodman, was the scourge of the American League.

June 23, 1950: The Boston Red Sox announced that Steve O'Neill (top) was going to be the new manager of the Red Sox, succeeding Joe McCarthy, who had resigned. O'Neill, a former Detroit and Cleveland manager, joined the Red Sox as a coach in the winter of 1949. McCarthy (bottom) previously managed the Chicago Cubs, the New York Yankees for 16 years, and the Sox from 1948 to 1950.

June 15, 1952: *The Red Sox signed the nation's top catching prospect, a former University of Florida quarterback, Haywood Sullivan. The 21-year-old Sullivan was signed for an estimated $75,000 bonus, with the Sox outbidding the Yankees for the rookie catcher. He only played in a few games and batted .150, but on May 23, 1980, this same former rookie catcher, along with team trainer Buddy LeRoux, became co-owners of the Boston Red Sox.*

March 2, 1955: *Jackie Jensen (left) and Jim Piersall, star outfielders for the Boston Red Sox, show young Kevin Cronin how they hold the bat. Kevin wears No. 9 for his favorite Red Sox player, Ted Williams. Kevin's dad is Joe Cronin, general manager of the Red Sox.*

In 1959, a young Notre Dame shortstop named Carl Yastrzemski signed a Red Sox contract. Two years later he replaced his idol Ted Williams in left field when Williams retired. In the 22 years that Yaz has worn a Red Sox uniform he has become a New England demigod and one of the greatest players in baseball. Yaz has won every conceivable batting title, numerous Gold Gloves for fielding supremacy, the MVP award, and is a Hall-of-Fame certainty when he becomes eligible.

Before the Goose (Gossage) there was the Monster. Dick Radatz was a 6-foot-7, 260-pound behemoth, who would come charging out of the bullpen at Fenway Park with a fastball that sent opposing batters running for cover. From 1962 through 1965 Radatz appeared in 207 games, struck out 487 batters, averaged 26 saves and 13 wins per season, and kept his earned-run average down around 2.00.

Two of Boston's all-time most prolific sluggers, Ted Williams (left) smashed 521 career home runs for the Red Sox and Dick Stuart crashed 75 in just 2 years (1963 and 1964).

Jim Lonborg was at his brilliant best during the 1967 season as he pitched the Red Sox to the American League Pennant and racked up a 22–9 record. He was voted the Cy Young Award as the best pitcher in the League, then went on in the World Series to climax a most successful year by beating the Cardinals twice in the Series. The Cardinals, however, captured the World Series from the valiant Red Sox.

Tom Yawkey purchased the Red Sox in 1933 and for 44 years he presided over the Red Sox like a doting father. Yawkey transformed the franchise into a New England institution and one of the biggest attractions in baseball. When he died in 1976 all of baseball mourned this fine sportsman. In this 1975 photo Yawkey offers some fatherly advice to one of his favorite ballplayers, Carl Yastrzemski.

October 10, 1975: Pitcher Luis Tiant and batterymate Carlton Fisk embrace after Tiant pitched a 3-hitter against the Oakland A's in the opening game of their playoff series. The Red Sox won, 7–1.

October 16, 1975: Boston catcher Carlton Fisk dives over the photographer's box in an attempt to catch a foul pop off the bat of the Reds' Tony Perez in the 6th inning of a World Series game under the watchful eyes of baseball Commissioner Bowie Kuhn (left, standing), National League President Chub Feeney (sitting) and Rogers Morton, Secretary of Commerce (right, standing).

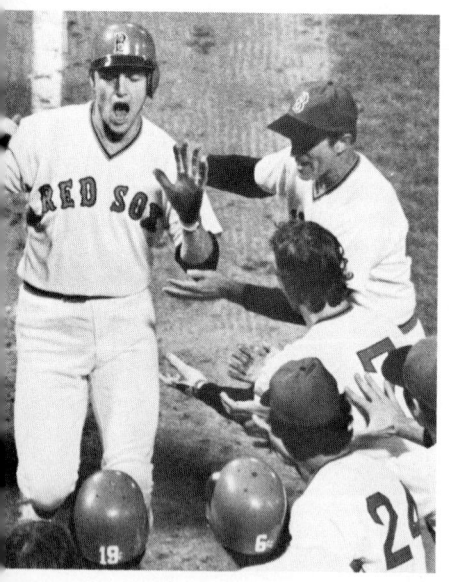

October 21, 1975, at Boston: The entire Red Sox bench greets catcher Carlton Fisk after he slammed the game-winning home run in the 12th inning of the 6th game of the World Series. The Sox won, 7–6, making the Series 3 games apiece, but the next day, October 22, the Cincinnati Reds defeated the Red Sox to win the Championship, 4 games to 3.

The 1975 Bosox battered the Oakland A's, sweeping the 3-game series to capture the American League Pennant. The World Series proved to be one of the most exciting in years as the Red Sox battled through 7 furiously tense contests. They lost to the Cincinnati Reds, 4–3, in the finale.

In 1975, the Red Sox put together one of the great young outfields in the American League: Jim Rice (left), Fred Lynn and Dwight Evans (right).

Signed as a free agent in 1978, fresh out of the College of the Sequoias, California, Bob Ojeda seems destined for future stardom. The hard-throwing left-hander had speed, a fine curveball and plenty of poise as he nearly pitched a no-hit game against the Yankees in the waning days of the 1981 season. Ojeda went into the 9th inning before allowing his first hit of the game. The Red Sox won 2–1, and the nation's sports pages extolled the finesse of the young hurler.

After a brilliant World Series performance in 1977, when he pitched and won 2 games for the Yankees against the Los Angeles Dodgers, Mike Torrez became a free agent and instant millionaire, when he signed a 7-year $2.7 million contract with the Boston Red Sox. A hard thrower, Torrez first came up to the major leagues with the St. Louis Cardinals in 1967.

Acquired from the Cleveland Indians in 1978, Dennis Eckersley quickly became the ace of the Bosox pitching corps. He won 20 games in 1978 and had 17 wins in 1979, but a bad back hampered Dennis in 1980, when he won 11 games and lost 14, for his first losing season. Despite the strike in 1981 Eckersley managed to win 10 games as the Sox battled to the very last day of the season for a playoff spot.

Ralph Houk was named manager of the Red Sox on October 27, 1980. A former Yankee manager, Houk led the Bronx Bombers to 3 straight pennants and 2 World Championships before he left to take over as manager of the Detroit Tigers. Houk had thought he was retiring from baseball in 1978 after 5 years with the Tigers. A former World War II hero of the Battle of the Bulge, Major Houk was awarded the Silver Star, the Bronze Star and the Purple Heart.

Carney Lansford, a .260 hitter for the California Angels in 1980, proved to be the player of the year in 1981 for the Red Sox as he smashed American League pitching for a .336 season average to lead all AL hitters. He went to the Sox on December 10, 1980, in a trade that sent Rick Burleson and Butch Hobson to the Angels for Lansford, pitcher Mark Clear and Rick Miller.

When Jerry Remy was injured in 1980, the Red Sox brought up Dave Stapleton from their Pawtucket farm club on May 20. Dave promptly took over at short and third, and filled in practically every position in the infield. He also hit for a .321 batting average and was high in the Rookie-of-the-Year voting as the season ended. Dave continued his solid play in '81 with a .282 average and seems on his way to stardom with the Bosox.

RED SOX TEAM PICTURE—The 1981 Red Sox are seen posing for the team picture at Boston's Fenway Park.

Chapter IV

FOR BASEBALL fans and American League left fielders, "the Green Monster"—the wall in left field—is either a chuckle or a nightmare, depending on one's point of view. Lots of cheap home runs have been popped in that direction, but then, back in 1912 when Fenway Park opened, the left-field area was a pitcher's and fielder's nemesis.

To begin with, the wall was not as high as its present thirty-seven feet, and the screen atop the wall wasn't installed until 1936. Next, the last twenty feet to the base of the wall had an embankment rising some ten feet or so. Many outfielders had problems; Bob Fothergill of the Tigers once rolled down the embankment, but Duffy Lewis got the hang of it early on, and played it so expertly that it became known as "Duffy's Cliff." It wasn't removed until Tom Yawkey renovated the park between 1933 and 1934.

The wall also proved to be a psychological barrier in another way, and it still is. Any major-league batter could reach it and go beyond; in fact, the first home run over the Monster was hit in late April, and the blow was struck by Hugh Bradley, a reserve first baseman—and his batting average that year was exactly .190. It looked so *damned easy* that right-handed batters went out of their minds trying to pull the ball, but pitchers then, as now, knew enough to keep the ball low and away, resulting in a bunch of groundouts.

The new park was inaugurated on April 9th with an exhibition game against Harvard, but the official opening was delayed by rain, including the twin bill scheduled for Patriots' Day. Some 27,000 fans showed up on April 20th, and enjoyed the proceedings immensely, as the Sox beat the Yankees in eleven innings, 7–6. Ordinarily, the victory would have received a lot of newspaper ink, but that was the day the *Titanic* sank.

How good were the Red Sox of 1912? Well, Connie Mack often called the Athletics of 1912 "my best team," but the A's never got within hailing distance of the Sox. The outfield of Duffy Lewis, Tris Speaker and Harry Hooper was probably the greatest outfield in baseball history. Larry Gardner at third base was the anchor. Ty Cobb never could bunt on him, and he couldn't understand his lack of success until years later, when Gardner told him he knew when the bunt was coming because Cobb locked his lips.

The pitching staff was far and away the best in the league, with Smokey Joe Wood, Buck O'Brien, Hugh Bedient, Ray Collins and "Sea Lion" Hall contributing to the team's total of 105 victories and .691 percentage, a record that stood until the Yankees of 1927 broke both marks with 110 wins and a .714 percentage.

The ace of the Red Sox pitching staff and one of the all-time pitching heroes of baseball, Joe Wood, was born in Kansas City on October 25, 1889, and by the time he was fifteen years old was known far and wide as "Smokey" Joe Wood, for his fast ball terrorized opposing batters and won him a reputation far beyond his young years. He pitched with success for the Hutchinson team of the old Western Association in 1907, and in 1908 he moved up to the Kansas City team. Toward the end of the 1908 season, Wood was sold to the Red Sox and appeared in two games, winning one, while losing one game. In 1909 Joe posted an 11-and-8 record. He won twelve games in 1910 and twenty-one games in 1911, including a no-hitter. In 1912 Joe Wood became the finest pitcher in baseball, winning an incredible thirty-four games, while losing but seven, including a skein of sixteen consecutive victories. In the 1912 World Series, Smokey Joe won three out of four games against the New York Giants, as the Red Sox went on to defeat the Giants four games to three to win the world championship.

There were heroes enough on the team, but if one star had to be singled out it was Tris Speaker. Called "Spoke" by his teammates, he was a former rodeo rider and telegraph lineman from Hubbard City, Texas. As an outfielder he was simply the best, nothing less. He played very shallow and it looked easy to pop one over his head, but he could run like a cheetah and his judgment of a fly ball was eerie. As Joe Wood said of him, "Spoke has that terrific instinct—at the crack of the bat he's off with his back to the infield, then he turns and glances back over his shoulder at the last minute. There's no one even in the same league with him."

Speaker also brutalized enemy pitching that year. He finished third in batting behind Ty Cobb and Joe Jackson with a .383 average, which included 222 hits.

Harry Hooper, in right field from 1909 to 1920, was perhaps almost on a par with Speaker defensively; at least Babe Ruth thought so. So did Joe Wood, who remarked, "Boy, if there was any one characteristic of Harry Hooper's, it was that he was a clutch player. When the chips were down he played like wildfire." Hooper wasn't as good a hitter as Speaker. He batted .300 only five times in his career and had a lifetime average of .281, but in the outfield, he considered spectacular catches all part of a day's work. He was a valuable leadoff man with great speed, and had one of the strongest throwing arms in baseball.

Duffy Lewis had come to Boston in 1910. A native of San Francisco, Duffy became a regular immediately. He played the left-field embankment at Fenway with such speed and skill that for generations afterwards, it was known as "Duffy's Cliff." The combination of Heinie Wagner and Steve Yerkes at short and second respectively was outstanding, with player-manager Jake Stahl rounding out the infield (plus Gardner, of course). A smart young catcher named Forrest Cady was a fine pickup from Newark.

On the mound Joe Wood reigned supreme. He won thirty-four and lost only five; his 258 strikeouts were second only to the 303 racked up by mighty Walter Johnson. Once, responding to a question, Johnson replied, "Can I throw harder than Joe Wood? Listen, my friend, there's no man alive can throw harder than Joe Wood." Oddly, both Wood and Johnson had sixteen-game winning streaks that season.

On September 6th, 1912, Joe Wood of Boston pitched against Walter Johnson of Washington. The fans expected a classic and they got it.

"The newspapers publicized us like prize fighters," Wood recalled later. "They gave statistics comparing our height, weight, biceps, triceps, arm span and whatnot. The champion, Walter Johnson, versus the challenger, Joe Wood. That was the only game I ever remember in Fenway Park, or anywhere else for that matter, where the fans were practically sitting along the first-base and third-base lines. Instead of sitting back where the bench usually was, we were sitting on chairs right up against the foul lines, and the fans were right behind us. Fenway must have had twice as many people as its seating capacity. The fans were on the field an hour before the game started, and it was so crowded down there I hardly had room to warm up."

Wood beat Johnson, 1–0. Johnson allowed five hits and fanned five, while Wood pitched a six-hitter and struck out nine. The only run of the game came in the sixth inning when Speaker belted one over third that went for a ground-rule double, and Duffy Lewis followed with a checked-swing blooper that plunked safely into right field, scoring Spoke.

Johnson had no greater admirer than Wood himself. "Johnson was the greatest pitcher who ever lived," Wood asserted. "If he'd ever had a good team behind him, what records he would have set!"

The Red Sox breezed home to win the American League flag by fourteen and a half games, and took on the powerful New York Giants in the World Series. The Giants had their own pitching ace in Rube Marquard, who'd won nineteen in a row, starting with the opening game of the season. Another dandy was rookie Jeff Tesreau, a hulking 220-pounder from Missouri, whose spitball helped him win seventeen games, and the great Christy Mathewson still had plenty left in his pitching arm. New York fans turned out in full force for the first game. By seven o'clock in the morning a line had formed that stretched down Eighth Avenue for twelve blocks.

Boston was well represented by the Royal Rooters. About a thousand fans, including Mayor John F. "Honey Fitz" Fitzgerald, boarded a train known as "the John Barleycorn Express," and made their presence known by parading through Times Square on the eve of the Series, singing a parody of the Tammany song. Later they marched around the Polo Grounds before the game, singing "Tessie" and "When I Get You Alone Tonight," while New Yorkers hissed and booed. Honey Fitz, in a black silk hat and stiff white collar, posed for pictures with any New York politician. The next afternoon, John F. Kennedy's grandfather presented Stahl and Speaker with new cars and gave Heinie Wagner a silver bat.

Manager John McGraw sprang a surprise on the Sox by starting Tesreau against Joe Wood. It really wasn't that much of a gamble, since Tesreau was the NL's earned-run leader that year, and McGraw wanted to hold Mathewson in reserve for the opener in Boston.

Wood was emotionally drained. Harry Hooper remembered how it was for the young pitcher. "The tension on Joe was just terrific all that season," Hooper said. "I was talking to him before one of the Series games and suddenly realized he couldn't say a word. The strain had started to get to him. But what could you expect? I think he was only twenty-two years old."

The Giants scored twice in the third on a walk, a Texas League double to short left and a line single to center by Red Murray. Boston answered with a run in the sixth on Speaker's liner to left center that might have been caught, but Snodgrass and Devore got their signals crossed as Devore cut in front of Snodgrass and had the ball deflect away. It went for a triple, and Speaker scored on an infield out.

In the seventh the Sox got lucky again. With one out and two on, Wood tapped a sure double-play grounder to second, but Larry Doyle couldn't find the handle and was barely able to make the force at second. Hooper's double and Yerkes's single accounted for three runs.

The Giants threatened in the ninth when, with one out, Merkle, Herzog and Meyers singled for a run. With the tying and winning runs on base, Wood fanned Fletcher and Crandall for his tenth and eleventh strikeouts of the game and the Red Sox had the game, 4–3.

Game two was a wild affair, pitting Mathewson against three Red Sox hurlers—Collins, Hall and Bedient—at Fenway, and Matty's luck was all bad. Five New York errors, including three by shortstop Art Fletcher, helped undo the Giants' southpaw. The game went eleven innings and ended in a 6–6 tie when darkness fell.

Game three had a controversial ending. Rube Marquard pitched a strong game and the Giants led, 2–1, in the ninth, but with two out the Sox had a pair of runners on base. Forrest Cady came to bat as darkness and mist settled in, making it almost impossible to see. Cady got a fat pitch and boomed a long, high drive to right center. Most of the fans couldn't follow the flight of the ball. All they saw were a couple of runners crossing the plate, and they assumed that Devore couldn't catch up with the long fly. But Devore made the out and continued running after he caught the ball, right into the clubhouse. Boston fans thought the game was won, 3–2, but it was New York's victory, 2–1.

Wood and Bedient won the next two games for the Red Sox by scores of 3–1 and 2–1. Stahl wanted to use Wood again to wrap up the Series, but club owner Jim McAleer had other ideas. He visited Stahl in his New York hotel room and asked, "Who are you pitching tomorrow?"

"Wood, of course," replied the surprised manager.

"Is that wise?" countered McAleer. "We're ahead, three games to one. Why not give Wood another day of rest and use O'Brien instead?"

Stahl tried to argue, but McAleer, using none too gentle words, reminded him that *he* was the president of the Red Sox, not Stahl. O'Brien pitched the next day.

In the first inning the game was over. With runners on the corners, O'Brien feinted a pickoff throw to first, and when he failed to complete the throw, umpire Bill Klem called the obvious balk and waved the runner home. O'Brien promptly collapsed. Two doubles and a single followed, scoring three runs, and then McGraw rubbed it in by calling a double steal. It worked too, even with Chief Meyers on first. Meyers was known far and wide as the slowest runner in the major leagues, and the Sox were probably startled to see the big Indian plodding toward second as fast as he could go. Yerkes made a wild throw to the plate and another run scored. The fifth run came across on another base hit. Lefty Collins pitched seven strong relief innings, but the Red Sox could only pick up two runs by then, and the Giants, behind Marquard, won, 5–2.

McAleer was a very unpopular man with the Boston players, and there were bitter feelings against him. Most of them said the same words: "Why the hell can't McAleer run his end and let Jake alone? If Wood had pitched, we'd be World Champions." O'Brien wasn't well liked either, and when he overheard some of the remarks about him he became belligerent. He got into a fist fight with Paul Wood, Joe's brother, who had bet a hundred dollars on the Sox. Paul hung a shiner on O'Brien that was reportedly a thing of beauty. It was an unhappy team that returned to Boston, and somehow the story spread that McAleer had ordered the change of pitchers because he wanted the gate receipts of a seventh game.

The next day brought about a near-riot even before a ball was pitched.

Very few people had expected more than three games in Boston. The Royal Rooters had bought a section of the left-field stands for those games and assumed they would be available for this game as well. However, Bob McRoy, who was in charge of ticket sales, had placed the seats on sale at the regular window and they were gone quickly. When the Royal Rooters marched onto the field before the game, they found their seats occupied.

There was hell to pay as Irish tempers flared. The umpires couldn't get the Rooters off the field, and neither could the foot police. Eventually, mounted cops were called in and they used force to do the job, shoving the enraged Royal Rooters behind the bleacher rail or out of the park completely. The scene was riotous and ugly. One soused Royal Rooter was seen leaning against a fence and yelling, "To hell with Queen Victoria!"—whatever that was supposed to mean. But a Boston newspaper compared the tactics of the mounted police with those used by Russian Cossacks.

The net result was harmful to Joe Wood. He had tried to warm up, but when the fans wouldn't get off the field he had to return to the dugout. It was a chilly day, and Wood had to sit there for half an hour. When play started his arm had stiffened, and he was shelled for half a dozen runs in the first inning. The Giants ran the Sox ragged on their way to a lopsided 11-4 win. With Bedient scheduled to face the mighty Mathewson for the eighth and final game, the Sox seemed to have little chance.

In the dugout before the game, Stahl approached Bedient and said, "Kid, you've got to win for us. Just pitch the way you did your last time out and you can beat Mathewson again." It was a tight game. The Giants scored in the third, and only Harry Hooper's incredible catch prevented another run from scoring. Devore clobbered one that Hooper barehanded, diving into the second row of the bleachers to take away a home run. The catch was actually illegal, since Hooper was entirely out of the playing field when he caught the ball, but that was a technicality the Red Sox fans totally ignored.

It was 1-0 into the seventh, with Matty turning away the Sox regularly. Then Stahl popped one into short left. The ball was surrounded by Devore, Snodgrass and Fletcher, but nobody thought to catch it and the bloop fell for a base hit. A walk moved Stahl to second, and with two out young Olaf Henriksen went in to pinch hit for Bedient. Matty got two strikes on him, then sent in a high outside curve. Olaf got enough wood on the ball to send a soft liner toward left. The ball hit third base and bounced into foul territory for a double. Stahl scored the tying run.

Joe Wood came in to pitch and he went into the tenth, yielding a run that put the Giants ahead, 2-1. Wood got the last out by knocking down a hard drive by Meyers, and could not have continued pitching if the game went longer.

Needing only three outs to win the World Series, Matty faced pinch hitter Clyde Engle, who hit a lazy fly to Snodgrass in center field. Snodgrass moved ten feet, camped under the ball—and dropped it! Engle pulled up at second. The unhappy Snodgrass tried to atone for the muff by making an outstanding catch on Harry Hooper's line drive, but there was something in the air now and Boston fans were warming to the occasion. Yerkes walked, bringing Speaker to the plate.

Mathewson bore down and Speaker popped a foul along the first-base line. Catcher Meyers, first baseman Merkle and pitcher Mathewson all went after it. Merkle should have stuffed the ball into his pocket, but for some reason he left it to the slow-moving Meyers. The ball dropped, Speaker was given another chance to hit, and he smacked the next pitch for a base hit that brought Engle home with the tying run, Yerkes taking third. To set up a force at any base, Duffy Lewis was intentionally walked. Larry Gardner put the game away with a long fly scoring Yerkes, and the Red Sox were champions.

The 1912 World Series became notorious as the one the Giants lost because Snodgrass dropped a fly ball, but that wasn't quite accurate. True, he permitted the tying run to get into scoring position, but what about the pop fly by Stahl that fell for a base hit, and the foul that wasn't caught because three players stared at the ball as if it were a UFO? In fact, to make Snodgrass feel better, he was given a raise the following season. But, since each winning Boston player received $4,024.68 and each losing Giant got $2,566.47, the 1912 fall classic went into history as "Snodgrass's thirty-thousand-dollar error."

Chapter V

THE BOSTON Red Sox fell from grace in 1913, finishing fourth with a 79–71 record. In part the slide was due to injuries: Joe Wood broke his thumb in spring training and was never the same pitcher again, perhaps because he tried to come back too soon and strained his arm; Stahl hurt his leg and became a part-time player; Heinie Wagner hurt his arm; Buck O'Brien wouldn't stay in shape and was sold to the White Sox.

The team was also rocked by dissension, especially because of the strained relations between Stahl and McAleer. Someone had started a rumor that Stahl would succeed McAleer as president. McAleer refused to listen to Stahl's denials and fired the manager early in July. The move angered Ban Johnson, Stahl's sponsor, who issued a statement saying that Jake had been "publicly humiliated." The papers featured a story that Johnson had "administered a stinging rebuke" to McAleer, who, in the interim, had turned the reins over to catcher Bill Carrigan as Stahl departed.

When William F. Carrigan graduated from Holy Cross College in 1907 and joined the Red Sox, his fellow players hung on him a *nom de diamond* which was apt and which stuck, both verbally and in print. One look at the lantern-jawed Irishman with the steely eyes and determined manner was enough to tag him for life as "Rough" Carrigan.

Carrigan came from Lewiston, Maine, where he had been a great baseball and football player in high school, and he car ried on in those sports for the Purple of Holy Cross, playing halfback under the demanding eye of Frank Cavanaugh, the Iron Major. Bill had come to Holy Cross as an infielder but the baseball coach at Worcester, Tommy McCarthy, noting his sturdy build and his catlike quickness, had made him over into a catcher.

It was as a catcher that Carrigan came to the Red Sox from Holy Cross and, as a catcher, Bill acquired his nickname. When Carrigan was sent to Toronto for further experience, he kicked like a steer. The next time Rough was to leave the Sox it was by his own volition, when he quit at the end of the 1916 season, after winning two successive World Championships, a feat which had been accomplished only twice before, by Frank Chance of the Cubs in 1907 and 1908 and by Connie Mack with the A's in 1910 and 1911.

Rough was only away from the Cross for seven years when he was named manager of the Sox in July 1913, succeeding Jake Stahl.

In Boston there was some speculation as to how the club would react to the firing of Stahl and the selection of Carrigan as the new manager. Speaker and Wood liked and respected their former manager, but they were professionals and never let personal feelings interfere with the way they played the game. Most of the others respected Carrigan, who was a rugged, intelligent man. He never let anyone get away with anything, whether teammate or member of the opposition.

Once, former umpire Billy Evans overheard a few words between Carrigan and another Red Sox player. "You're no better than anyone else on the club," Carrigan bellowed. "When I give an order for morning practice, you be there. I don't care how well you're playing, there will be discipline on this club, and I'm the guy to enforce it."

Then came the sound of a scuffle, followed by silence. Evans asked what had happened and was told, "Nothing much. Bill just grabbed one of the boys who wouldn't listen to reason. He'll behave now."

Larry Gardner told the story of Detroit's George Moriarty reaching first base safely and calling back to Carrigan, "Hey, you Irish SOB, I'm coming around the bases and knock you on your back." Moriarty did have that opportunity. He banged into Carrigan, but it was Moriarty who was stretched flat. Carrigan looked down at Moriarty, spat tobacco juice near his head and growled, "How do you like that, you Irish SOB?"

One bright spot in Boston's 1913 season was the defensive play of outfielders Lewis, Speaker and Hooper. That year they set a record of eighty-four assists which still stands. They played together for six years and accounted for 455 assists. Also, in 1913, Speaker batted .365.

Meanwhile, Ban Johnson was still seething over McAleer's dismissal of Stahl, and Boston fans had never forgiven Bob McRoy's ticket mixup of 1912. In fact, Mayor Fitzgerald had already called upon the league to get rid of McRoy. So, while McAleer was on a worldwide goodwill tour, Johnson announced that the Red Sox had been sold after the 1913 season to a New York hotel and real estate magnate named Joseph J. Lannin.

Lannin was a self-made millionaire. Born in Quebec, he first came to Boston at the age of fifteen and took a job as a bellhop. A thrifty soul with a good head for business, he saved his money religiously, and by the time he purchased the Red Sox for $200,000, he already owned the Great Northern Hotel in New York, the Garden City Hotel, a few golf courses on Long Island and an assortment of other valuable properties. Once he had owned a piece of the Boston Braves, and at the time of the Red Sox purchase Lannin had been trying vainly to buy the Philadelphia Phillies. According to the deal, the Taylors still kept a big interest in the Red Sox as well as the bonds on Fenway Park. Boston sportswriter A.H.C. Mitchell took over McRoy's job. Joseph J. Lannin took over a headache.

Part of the problem was the new Federal League which had just been formed. The new group was in open competition for the established stars of the American and National Leagues, some of whom had been on the world tour with McAleer, John McGraw, Charles Comiskey and others. Among the players were Speaker, Fred Merkle, Sam Crawford, Larry Doyle, Buck Weaver, Lee Magee, Otto Knabe and Mickey Doolan. As the players came off the Cunard liner, a small army of Federal League agents surrounded them waving contracts.

Several major-leaguers had already jumped to the new league, notably Joe Tinker of Tinker-to-Evers-to-Chance fame. From the Cunard's passenger list only Magee and the Phillies' keystone combination of Knabe and Doolan were signed, but the repercussions were widespread. Competition for players hiked salaries tremendously. For instance, in 1913, Speaker had earned nine thousand dollars. Now he demanded and received a two-year contract calling for $36,000.

When the Federal League placed clubs in International League cities, the results almost caused the old minor league to fold. Baltimore was in bad financial straits and had to sell some of its best players. During the 1914 season, Connie Mack was offered three stars, catcher Ben Egan, plus southpaws Ernie Shore and Babe Ruth. Mack had little money to spare and told Baltimore owner Jack Dunn, "Sell them to somebody who can pay you real money for them." Dunn approached Lannin, and in early July sold him the trio for eight thousand dollars. The price tag on Babe Ruth was $2,900. Later, Ruth was to say of Carrigan, "He was the best manager I ever played for."

There is nothing anyone can add to the well-known story of Babe Ruth, except perhaps for some interesting aspects of his early life in Baltimore as an "incorrigible" boy and his incredible success as one of baseball's greatest pitchers in the early 1900s.

George Herman Ruth was born on February 7th, 1895, in a small wooden frame house on Emory Street in Baltimore. Although the house is now a museum that houses Babe Ruth's memoirs and is open to the public, Ruth lived there only until his mother was strong enough after his birth to return to her mother's home on Frederich Avenue.

By the time little George was six years old the father had taken his family and moved several times, finally settling in a house on West Camden Street, where they lived over a saloon that Ruth Senior opened.

The family worked long, tedious hours in the saloon and had little time for the husky, aggressive, active young George. He avoided school, roamed the streets with a tough little gang and became more and more difficult to control.

"I was a real little bum when I was a kid," said Ruth.

Finally, the family, unable to control him, committed Ruth to St. Mary's School, an industrial school and home for "incorrigibles."

St. Mary's was run by the Xaverian Brothers, a Catholic order, but received financial support from the City of Baltimore and from the State, and took in boys from other religions. Singer Al Jolson was a St. Mary's alumnus.

The boys received religious training, regular classroom work and a strong dose of industrial training and, since most of them were hyperactive, there were many athletic activities; baseball, football and basketball. Ruth participated in all sports, but it was baseball that he really loved, and it occupied all of his spare time. He played the game and followed the reports of the big-league teams with great and excited interest.

Although Brother Paul, a small, neat man, was the head of St. Mary's, the boys referred to Brother Mathias, a huge, six-foot, six-inch giant of a man, as the boss of the school.

Ruth caught Brother Mathias's attention early, and the calm, considerate attention the big man gave the hell-raising kid struck a strong response in the boy's soul. He further endeared himself to Ruth by patiently batting out long fungos to the boys, hour after hour. Later, Brother Mathias would take Ruth aside and work with him, hitting grounder after grounder to the boy.

"I could hit the ball real good," said Ruth later, "and I could hit the first time I picked up a bat. But Brother Mathias made me a good fielder and taught me some real baseball stuff."

As the years rolled on at St. Mary's, Ruth, primarily a left-handed catcher, took to pitching because of his size. He threw left-handed, and could throw the ball harder than anyone at the school.

Among the many brothers who guided the destinies of the boys at St. Mary's was a Brother Gilbert. He had been watching Ruth for nearly a decade and saw that the boy was an absolute baseball fanatic. Baseball was all that could hold Ruth's attention, and Gilbert recognized not only his single-minded devotion to the game, but also his exceptional gifts and ability. Brother Gilbert realized that Ruth had the skill to become a professional ballplayer.

It was about this time that Gilbert decided to write a letter to a friend, Jack Dunn, manager of the Baltimore Orioles. Finally, after several letters, Dunn came out to St. Mary's. He saw George and liked what he saw. To those of us who remember Ruth only when he was established as a major-league home-run hitter, it is hard to picture the boy Dunn saw that day at "the Home," as St. Mary's was known.

To begin with, Ruth was a kid. He was about seventeen, tall and gangly, painfully thin almost everywhere except across his chest and shoulders, which even then were showing signs of massiveness.

At St. Mary's, Ruth pitched for Dunn. He was not dressed in baseball flannels, but wore a pair of blue denim overalls, which was standard dress for all the boys. Dunn saw Ruth pitch for about half an hour and was satisfied with his efforts.

After the workout Brother Gilbert said, "What do you think about George?"

Dunn drew a deep breath and said, "What do you want for him, Brother?"

"John, he isn't mine to sell. All I want for him is a good home, proper care and the chance for him to make good and to be somebody in this world, no more and no less."

Dunn and the brother talked at great length after that modest speech. Jack Dunn then arranged to sign formal papers acting as Ruth's guardian, and to pay the boy a salary of six hundred dollars for the 1914 season. George Ruth was to be Dunnie's ward and responsibility first, and a southpaw for the Orioles afterward.

Ruth took Dunn's guardianship literally, for when the Orioles assembled for training at Fayetteville, North Carolina, a few weeks later, he trotted puppylike onto the practice field following Dunn. Big George resembled a puppy in more ways than one—he was a growing kid, he was awkward and, above all, he was terribly anxious to please.

It was on this first day of practice that Ruth was to draw the nickname which was to stick to him for all the days and years of his life. Hal Stienman was a coach for the Orioles and

Dunn's assistant on the field, and when Ruth arrived on the field at Fayetteville that day in March 1914, trotting along after Dunn, it was Stienman who said, "Here comes Jack Dunn with his newest babe."

It was Babe from that day on.

At Fayetteville, Ruth was one of the greenest kids ever on a training trip. He was amazed at the amount and variety of food and stuffed himself daily to the bursting point. He almost had his head taken off riding up and down elevators, and he fell for every prank the older players rigged for him. To get him away from the men and to protect him, Dunnie had Ruth room with Roger Pippen, then a smart young sportswriter for the *Baltimore News Post*.

"At Fayetteville," said Ruth, "Dunnie saw to it that we took things easy for a long time, and when we did finally have a game it was one of those intrasquad games. Dunnie picked the teams. One was the Sparrows and the other the Buzzards. I played shortstop for the Buzzards for half the game and then finished by pitching.

"Late in that game I hit the first professional home run of my life. The ball cleared the right-field fence and landed in a cornfield beyond and Dunnie and the rest of the guys were amazed at the carry of my hit."

However, it was Ruth's pitching, rather than his hitting, that made the headlines. In preseason games in Carolina and in Baltimore, against the World Champion Athletics, the Giants and the Phillies, young Babe Ruth breezed through such great hitters as Frank Baker, Eddie Collins, Larry Doyle, Red Murray and Sherry Magee as though they were schoolboy opponents at St. Mary's. He hung up a long string of early shutout innings and impressed all who saw him pitch.

John McGraw was so impressed with Ruth that he contacted Dunn and said, "Jack, that young left-hander you had out there today looked very good. Whenever you're ready to put Ruth on the market, I want you to give me first crack at him." McGraw always insisted Jack had agreed, but Dunnie was having many financial worries then and didn't pay too much attention to McGraw's remarks.

Babe Ruth became a star as soon as the season opened. On

April 22nd, 1914, he made his first start as an Oriole and shut out a strong Buffalo team, 6–0. Playing second base for Buffalo that day was Joe McCarthy, who went 0-for-4 against Ruth. The Buffalo catcher was Paul Kritchell, who in later years became a great Yankee scout. Ruth drove out two singles in his three times at bat.

The Federal League had by this time muscled in on Dunn's territory and built a ball park directly across the street from the Orioles' park, and the Feds opened their season a day before the Orioles. On opening day the new Federal League club drew more than twenty thousand spectators, while the best that the Orioles could draw was a mere five thousand fans.

One day the Orioles drew less than fifty people to the ball park, and Dunn decided he had to sell his players. Babe Ruth, Ernie Shore and catcher Ben Egan went to the Boston Red Sox for $8,500, and a new era had begun.

The Ruth sale was completed July 8th. Babe stayed with the Red Sox for a month, during which he won two games and lost one. Joe Lannin, the owner of the Red Sox, then sent Ruth to Providence to help Bill Donovan win the International League pennant. And Babe turned the trick with a late-season display of near-shutout pitching. Even though he missed a month of International League ball, Ruth's record with the Orioles and Providence was twenty-two victories and nine defeats.

The American League season still had a week to go, and the Red Sox, well out of the pennant race, recalled Ruth. In Boston he pitched against the Yankees and won, 11–5, and had his first major-league hit, a double off Len Cole. A few days later in a game with Washington he pinch hit against the great Walter Johnson and struck out. On the final day of the season, the Babe pitched the middle three innings (he was not involved with the decision), came to bat once and drove out a single.

Thus ended the extraordinary rookie year of Babe Ruth. Just out of a boys' home for incorrigibles, he won fourteen games by July 6th with the Orioles and was a key factor in helping the club take a commanding lead in the International League pennant race. At Providence he won nine games and helped his club down the stretch to win the pennant from his former club, the Orioles.

In 1915 a rookie trying to break into the lineup of a major-league team had a difficult time with his teammates. Ballplayers in those days were rugged individuals who battled newcomers and each other fiercely with words and actions. A rookie coming to the majors was hazed and insulted unmercifully. When Ruth tried to take his turn at the Red Sox practice he had to fight for a spot. The next morning, when he came to his locker in the clubhouse, he found his bats sawed neatly into sections.

Until his later years, when he grew broodingly bitter over the inescapable fact that professional baseball had closed and bolted the doors on him, Ruth had the happy faculty of wearing the world as a loose garment. His unhappy childhood, his years at "the Home" all faded behind him. The closed circle the Red Sox presented to the Babe didn't worry him an iota. They could have sawed up all the bats that ever came out of Louisville, but they couldn't freeze out the Babe.

Within a year, Ruth was one of the Red Sox gang. At nineteen he had a car and a new wife, a sixteen-year-old waitress named Helen Woodford. They went on bowling parties with the other Red Sox players and their wives, notably Jack Barry and Mrs. Barry, a schoolteacher.

When Ruth was purchased by Joe Lannin for Boston, Bill Carrigan—Old Rough—wasted no time in getting a look at him. Tradition has it that the Babe, after a sleepless night on the train from Baltimore to Boston, was started in a game against Cleveland the very day he arrived. He won his first American League game by a 4–3 score.

In 1914 Babe Ruth won two games and lost one for the Sox, but it was just the beginning of a long and glorious career. In 1915 he became one of the most effective pitchers on the fine Red Sox squad as he won eighteen games while losing but eight. And in 1916 Ruth had the best pitching record for the Bosox with twenty-three and twelve. In 1917 it was twenty-four and thirteen. He was thirteen and seven in 1918, but by this time he was spending more time in the outfield and wielding that big bat of his when not pitching. He was nine and five in 1919, but his pitching days were just about over as he played in 130 games and slugged a record twenty-nine home runs. His .322 batting average and his colorful long-distance drives added tremendous excitement in every game he played. He could not be just a pitcher. He had to be in the lineup every day. The crowd wanted it that way and so did his manager.

The Red Sox improved noticeably in 1914, finishing in second place. In 1915 they went all the way, beating the Detroit Tigers for the flag. The Red Sox mound corps was solid. George Foster was 20–9, Shore racked up a 19–7 record, Ruth was 18–8, Dutch Leonard posted a 15–7 log. In the bullpen were two kid pitchers named Herb Pennock and Carl Mays, both future greats.

During the World Series against the NL-champion Phillies, Lannin used Braves Field as the home arena. The previous year, while their new park was being built, "the Miracle Braves of 1914" had used Fenway. Braves Field had eight thousand more seats, which was as good a reason as any for the switch by the AL club.

Carrigan didn't think much of the Phils. They had a couple of great players, particularly Grover Cleveland Alexander (later portrayed in film by Ronald Reagan), who had won thirty-one games, twelve by shutout, and had an ERA of 1.22. Also, slugger Gavvy Cravath, who had hit a record twenty-four home runs. Carrigan told his men, "The Phillies aren't half the team McGraw had three years ago, and we beat 'em. Now, this Alexander can be tough. He's one of the best in baseball, and when we face him, our pitchers have to get a shutout or limit them to one run. We might have to face him three times if the Series goes long enough, so let's keep bearing down."

Shore faced Alex in game one and the Sox lost, 3–1. All the runs scored in the game were cheap, resulting from Texas League bloopers, infield hits, errors of commission and omission and just bad baseball.

The second game was another pitching duel, matching Foster with Erskine Mayer. The Sox scored first when Hooper and Speaker engineered a double steal although, oddly enough, neither player was credited with a stolen base. The

Phils tied it with back-to-back doubles by Cravath and first baseman Fred Luderus, but never threatened again. Foster drove in the winning run in the ninth with his third hit of the game, and while Milt Stock threw a scare into the Red Sox with a long drive toward the bleachers, Speaker made one of his patented spectacular catches to ensure the 2–1 Boston win. That game, played in Baker Bowl on October 9th, was historic in a sense, for it marked the first time a president of the United States attended a World Series game. President Woodrow Wilson threw out the first ball.

Dutch Leonard outpitched Alexander in the third game as Boston won in the ninth, 2–1. Alexander allowed only six hits, Leonard gave up three. Game four had the same result with the same score, Boston winning, 2–1. The numbers had been repeated with such regularity that the 1915 World Series became known as the "Two-to-One Series." This time Ernie Shore bested George "Dut" Chalmers, a spitball pitcher who had learned his trade on the sandlots of Harlem.

Babe Ruth never did pitch in the 1915 World Series. Foster got the nod for the fifth game, and although he didn't have his usual stuff, the Sox took the game, 5–4, the winning margin coming on two home runs by Harry Hooper into the temporary bleachers erected in the Baker bandbox. The homer hit by Duffy Lewis was an authentic four-master. The Red Sox were the World Champions, and the reason, according to Ty Cobb, who covered the games as a reporter, was the tight Boston defense.

The World Championship of 1915, combined with the demise of the Federal League, proved to be a mixed blessing for Joe Lannin. Since there was no competition for athletes, Lannin wanted to cut Speaker's eighteen-thousand-dollar salary, pointing out that Speaker wasn't hitting as well any longer. From his .383 high in 1912, Tris had "slumped" in successive years, to .366, .338 and .322. The center fielder refused. Joe Wood, faced with a cut down to five thousand dollars, also got his hackles up. Although he wasn't signed, Speaker worked out in spring training with the club, but Wood would not come to camp.

As a harbinger of things to come, Lannin purchased from

the St. Louis Browns a center fielder named Clarence "Tilly" Walker, a dependable outfielder who could hit for extra bases but was certainly no Speaker, neither in the field nor at bat. Then Ban Johnson got into the act. Johnson owned a piece of the Cleveland Indians, a team recently taken over by his friend, Jim Dunn. With the help of Johnson, Dunn swung a deal, trading pitcher "Sad Sam" Jones, infielder Fred Thomas and fifty thousand dollars for Tris Speaker. Wood was also later acquired by Cleveland, and the former pitching great was turned into an outfielder. Boston fans were amazed—and some were enraged—but the deal was made and there was no calling it back. Sam Jones was to have an outstanding major-league career, and Speaker showed up his old boss by reversing the decline in his batting average, leading the league with a gaudy .386.

Yet Boston won the AL flag and the World Series against Brooklyn in 1916. It was the pitching staff that did it, a staff featuring a growing boy named Babe Ruth, who blossomed into the best left-hander in the American League, posting a 23–12 record with a 1.75 ERA. Leonard won eighteen, Shore and Carl Mays each won seventeen, Foster had fourteen wins. Both Leonard and Shore hurled no-hitters. Brooklyn fell in five games, one of which went fourteen innings with Ruth winning, 2–1. The infield was a stone wall, particularly Everett "Deacon" Scott at shortstop. Brooklyn manager Wilbert Robinson, observing Scott's "trolley line" throws from deep short, moaned, "Whenever things got going good for us, we'd go out on that trolley line."

Bill Carrigan had announced late in the season that he was going to retire from baseball. The insiders thought he was merely sounding off to squeeze more money out of Lannin, but Rough Carrigan meant it, and when the last ball was pitched, he went home to Maine and the banking business. George Foster, once a mainstay of the Boston staff, also packed his glove away for good. A decade later, however, Carrigan would be talked out of retirement to return as manager of the Red Sox, but not for long.

Joe Lannin was tired of constantly arguing with Ban Johnson, and his health was failing. He had hinted that he was thinking of selling the club, and when he did, there were those who thought he did so just to annoy Johnson. However, the *Boston American* reported a sale price of better than a million dollars.

The new owners were a pair of theatrical men from New York, Harry Frazee and Hugh J. Ward. The team had been purchased with a down payment and the promise to pay some $400,000 out of profits in three years. Infielder Jack Barry, a popular man out of Holy Cross, as Carrigan had been, was named manager.

World War I did not hamper baseball in 1917. The Sox played about as well as they had the previous season but finished second, nine games behind the White Sox. Babe Ruth not only won twenty-three games but showed signs of becoming a fine hitter. He hit .325 with two homers in fifty-two games. Babe and Ernie Shore participated in one of the strangest games ever played.

On June 23rd, against Washington, Ruth started by walking the leadoff man. Ruth later recalled, "Three of the four balls should have been strikes. I growled some, but when he called the fourth ball, I just went crazy."

Ruth called umpire Brick Owen a blind bat and came off the mound. Owen told him to go back to the mound and pitch. Ruth stormed to the plate and hollered, "If you'd go to bed at night, you so-and-so, you could keep your eyes open long enough in the daytime to see a ball when it goes over the plate."

"Shut up, you lout," snapped Owen, "or I'll throw you out of the game."

"Throw me out and I'll punch you right in the jaw," Ruth roared.

Owen jerked his thumb. "You're out of the game right now," the ump said, raising his voice.

As Ruth described the action, "I hauled off and hit him, but good. It wasn't a love tap. I really socked him."

Jack Barry, the second baseman and manager, sprinted to the bench and called to Shore, "Get in there and stall until I can get somebody warmed up."

Shore, who died in 1980, recalled, "What he wanted me to

do was go out on the mound and kill as much time as possible while he got someone else ready in the bullpen. But there wasn't much stalling I could do, because when a pitcher was thrown out of the game, the next man was entitled to just five warmup pitches."

Shore, who was just coming off a suspension because of a fight in Chicago, warmed up hastily, and on his first delivery to the plate, the runner tried to steal second. He was thrown out by catcher Sam Agnew. When the inning was over, Barry asked Shore if he wanted to continue. Shore felt good, his curveball was breaking, his arm was loose. He nodded, went to the bullpen and warmed up a little more.

"From then on," Shore said, "I don't think I could have worked easier if I'd been sitting in a rocking chair. I think I threw seventy-five pitches the entire game. They kept hitting it at somebody. Only one ball was hit hard, in the ninth, but Duffy Lewis got it in left field."

It was a bizarre perfect game, won by Boston, 4–0. After that walk nobody else got on, and the runner was erased, so that only twenty-seven Senators came to bat. As for Ruth, he was suspended for one week and fined a hundred dollars. Today he might be suspended for a year, or even banned from the game for hitting an umpire.

After the 1917 season was over, baseball players were inducted into the services in droves. The Red Sox lost Frank Barry, Duffy Lewis, Shore, Del Gainer, Pennock, Thomas, Jim Walsh, Hal Janvrin, Chick Shorten, Mike McNally and a number of others. After pitching sixteen games, Dutch Leonard also changed uniforms. Frazee, who had money then, wheeled and dealed, acquiring from Connie Mack such stalwarts as first baseman Stuffy McInnis, outfielder Amos Strunk, catcher Wally Schang and pitcher "Bullet" Joe Bush.

The war did strange things to baseball in general and to the Red Sox in particular. The season was shortened to end on Labor Day, and with special permission from War Secretary Newton D. Baker, the World Series was played, ending on September 16th. Babe Ruth was moved to left field when he wasn't pitching, with the result that he hit .300 with twenty-six doubles, eleven triples and eleven homers (the eleven home runs tying him for the league lead). Ruth also won thirteen games with his pitching. The ace of the pitching staff was Carl Mays, with a 21–13 record.

Edward Grant Barrow, a veteran baseball man with major and minor league experience with Toronto, Montreal, Indianapolis, Patterson and the Detroit Tigers, replaced Jack Barry as manager. Barrow was a rough and tough baseball man and ruled the Red Sox with an iron hand. There were several run-ins and incidents with Babe Ruth, and then one day Barrow ordered Ruth into his office, locked the door, peeled off his shirt, put up his fists and said, "Ruth, now, I've had it with you. Put your dukes up or get the hell out of here and obey orders." And the Babe meekly got up, opened the door and walked out. He gave Barrow no trouble thereafter. Years later, Ed Barrow joined the Yankees' front office and as general manager helped put together the great Yankee teams of the late 1920s, 1930s and 1940s.

Under the tough guidance of Ed Barrow, the Red Sox won the American League flag and went head-to-head with the Chicago Cubs. It was a typical Red Sox Series, in that all the scores were low. Babe Ruth won two games by scores of 1–0 and 3–2. Carl Mays won the other two by scores of 2–1 and 2–1. The Red Sox won the World Championship four games to two.

"The War to End All Wars" was over less than two months after the World Series ended. Nobody could foresee the *exact* future of the Boston Red Sox, but perhaps, if an expert soothsayer had taken the trouble to go into a trance, that sage might have predicted not only the falling of the Red Sox, but also the rise of the New York Yankees. In a true sense it can be said that while Colonel Jake Ruppert, the beer mogul who owned the Yankees, turned his team into a great dynasty, he was aided and abetted by a gentleman named Harry Frazee, who, for a few years more, owned the Boston Red Sox.

Chapter VI

THE DISMANTLING of the Boston team—sometimes described as "the Rape of the Red Sox"—began shortly after the 1918 season. The boys were coming back from the service and suddenly Harry Frazee found that the club had a surplus of valuable baseball players, some getting too difficult to handle and drawing handsome salaries besides.

Boston fans were aghast to learn, one fine morning, that Frazee had sold Ernie Shore, Dutch Leonard and Duffy Lewis, their new destination being New York City. In return, the Sox received some warm bodies named Walters, Caldwell, Love and Gilhooley. To be fair to Frazee, neither Shore nor Lewis had ever returned to prewar form, while Leonard subsequently got into a salary dispute with Colonel Ruppert and was sent off to Detroit.

Meanwhile, Frazee was having his own problems with Babe Ruth, who wanted a tremendous salary increase, much more then Frazee could afford to pay. Ruth went so far as to hire a manager and threaten to quit baseball in favor of boxing, but in the end he signed a three-year Red Sox contract for ten thousand dollars annually. Ruth had a fine year in 1919, but the Red Sox didn't. Neither did Frazee.

Ruth hit twenty-nine home runs that season, playing mostly in the outfield. The switch from pitcher was practically mandatory. Ruth was a box office attraction, and pitching him once or twice a week was meaningless. In the outfield he could play every day. More people would come to see him in action, and Frazee needed cash desperately. Ruth obliged the fans with his home-run production, four of which were grand slams.

Carl Mays was another migraine for Frazee. After winning twenty-two in 1917 and twenty-one in 1918, he suddenly lost his effectiveness and by mid-July he was 5–11. Perhaps Mays was paranoid and thought his teammates weren't putting out when he was on the mound, but he seemed to have made his point on July 13th when the Sox made several errors behind him. He walked off the field between innings, saying, "I'll never pitch another game for the Red Sox." Ed Barrow sent someone after him, but Mays had already dressed. "Tell Barrow I've gone fishin'," were the last words he said as a member of the Red Sox.

Any number of clubs put in offers for the submarine ace, but Ban Johnson was not about to let Mays get away. Johnson was livid when, on July 29th, Frazee sold Mays to the Yankees for forty thousand dollars and a couple of pitchers named Russell and McGraw. Johnson issued a statement to the press:

"Baseball cannot tolerate such a breach of discipline. . . . Mays should have been suspended for breaking his contract. . . . It is now my duty as head of the American League to act. Mays will not play with any club until the suspension is raised."

The Yankee owners got an injunction restraining Johnson, and suddenly the whole league was split into two factions, one composed of Frazee, Ruppert and Comiskey, of the White Sox, the other consisting of Johnson and "the Loyal Five," meaning the rest of the league. Suits and countersuits flew back and forth, and for a while Johnson refused to recognize the games pitched by Mays as part of the official records. Eventually Johnson had to bite the bullet: the lawsuits were called off and a temporary truce was arranged.

However, the bitterness could not be easily erased. As part of major league baseball, the National League had to get involved in the fracas, and Johnson had become a mighty unpopular man. As a result, Kenesaw Mountain Landis was named high commissioner of both leagues, and there was nothing Johnson could do about it, as the National League threatened to form a twelve-team organization with two clubs in Boston, New York and Chicago.

Boston had finished sixth in 1919, and the future looked bleak for Frazee. Thus, on January 9th, 1920, Jake Ruppert of the Yankees told New York reporters:

"Gentlemen, we have just bought Babe Ruth from Harry Frazee of the Boston Red Sox. I can't give the exact figures, but it was a pretty big check—six figures. No players are involved. It is strictly a cash deal."

Ruppert did not tell the whole story at that time, but eventually it leaked out. Ruth's purchase price of $100,000 was a minor part of the transaction. Lannin was still waiting for his money and Frazee couldn't pay. What Ruppert did was take a $350,000 mortgage on Fenway Park so that Frazee could pay off some debts.

Ed Barrow had fought tooth and nail against the deal. "You can't do this to me, Harry," he screamed. "Ruth is the biggest attraction in baseball."

"I'm sorry, I've got to do it," Frazee replied softly. Later he told a sportswriter, "The Ruth deal was the only way I could retain the Red Sox." And he also pointed out that Ruth's twenty-nine home runs did not keep the Red Sox out of sixth place.

The Sox battled hard in 1920 but could finish no higher than fifth. About all the team had was pitching, getting sixteen wins from Herb Pennock, fifteen from Joe Bush and thirteen from Sam Jones. A fresh young rookie named Waite Hoyt chipped in with six. At the end of the year Ed Barrow was gone, becoming general manager of the New York Yankees.

As the years passed the Red Sox traded or sold more than a dozen Red Sox stars to the Yankees. Before the 1921 season, Frazee sent away Wally Schang, Waite Hoyt and a couple of others, and the key man he got in return was catcher Herold "Muddy" Ruel. Manager Miller Huggins didn't want to part with Ruel, but he had big eyes for the Schang-Hoyt battery. The trade gave the Yanks their first pennant as Red Sox castoffs delivered the goods. Ruth hit fifty-nine home runs, Carl Mays won twenty-seven and Hoyt won nineteen. The Red Sox finished fifth again under manager Hugh Duffy.

The Boston-New York relationship became one of the most intriguing in baseball history. Since Joe Bush had won sixteen and Sam Jones had won twenty-three in 1921, it was only natural for Ruppert to wave some money at Frazee and get them into Yankee uniforms. It was a complicated four-way deal in which the Yanks got Jones, Bush and shortstop Everett Scott for pitchers Jack Quinn, Warren Collins and Bill Piercy and shortstop Roger Peckinpaugh, once the Yankee captain. Peckinpaugh was promptly sent to Washington for the former Athletics shortstop, Joe Dugan. Washington got Dugan in the first place by sending Connie Mack outfielder Bing Miller and a Cuban pitcher named Acosta.

But Ruppert wasn't finished yet that year. When the St. Louis Browns threatened to win the flag, Ruppert sent a bundle of money to Frazee (with some players, of course, to make it look more palatable), and Dugan was in a Yankee uniform. After each transaction, Hugh Duffy would say loyally, "There were only players involved, no other consideration." And the *Boston Traveler*'s John Drohan would slyly write, "Oh, well, another of Frazee's road companies will eat for a few weeks."

Actually, Frazee's Broadway musicals were losing money regularly. He did produce *No, No, Nanette*, which was a hit, but then came some highly forgettable shows, such as *The Kissing Girl, A Pair of Sixes* and *My Lady Friends*. These shows had posters stuck on Fenway's outer walls, and one fan, looking at the billboard, remarked, "Those are the only friends that son-of-a-bitch Frazee has."

The Dugan deal aroused the wrath of almost everyone, including the folks in St. Louis, whose Browns had almost taken the pennant until Jumping Joe came along to play third for the Yankees. The complaint was not lost on Judge Landis, and after the season was over, he established June 15th of each season as the trading deadline.

It was in 1922 that the Yankees were beaten by the New York Giants in the World Series. Miller Huggins, the scrappy Yankee skipper, knew what was wrong. The Yanks had the best of Boston's pitching in Mays, Hoyt, Bush and Jones, but they were all right-handers. "What we need is a good southpaw to stop those left-handed hitters," he told Ruppert.

By then there was only one established left-hander in Boston, the great Herb Pennock. Frazee dutifully sent Pennock to New York, where he became one of the league's best pitchers. To compound the felony, a promising young minor-league pitcher was soon making the trip from South Carolina to New York, courtesy of Harry Frazee. The kid's name was George Pipgras, who also became a big winner for Ruppert. And so, when the New York Yankees won the World Series in 1923, of their twenty-four roster players, eleven had come from the Red Sox.

That year was also Harry Frazee's swan song in baseball. On April 18th, 1923, when the new Yankee Stadium was unveiled, Frazee marched with Ruppert to center field for the ceremony. Then, sitting with Ruppert in a box in "the House that Ruth Built," Frazee watched his old employees beat his Sox, 4–1. The Babe hit his first Stadium home run.

In July Frazee sold out to St. Louis business manager Bob Quinn. Frazee died six years later. Perhaps it was only fitting and proper that New York's dapper mayor, Jimmy Walker, should be at Frazee's bedside as he gasped his life away.

In 1918, Harry Frazee's team had been the World Champions. The Red Sox would not see the first division again until 1934 and would finish last six seasons in succession. Attendance plummeted with the team's standing. From 1927 through 1933, which was Tom Yawkey's first year as owner, the Sox drew a total of fewer fans than they did in 1979 alone.

Managers paraded into and out of Fenway. Frank Chance tried the job in 1923 after managing the Cubs and Yankees, but he lasted only a year. Next came Lee Fohl, and after him Bill Carrigan returned. Rough lasted three years and finished last each year. He was succeeded by John Collins, who hung around for about a year and a half.

The trades continued, some good, most of them bad. A good trade was the acquisition of Howard Ehmke from the Tigers, a trade manager Ty Cobb called his worst. On September 7th, 1923, Ehmke pitched a no-hitter against Philadelphia, but Ehmke was lucky, since Slim Harriss didn't touch first base after his drive off the wall and was called out, and Mike Menoskey was given an error when he couldn't hold a hard line drive. In Ehmke's next start he faced the Yankees, and the leadoff batter, Whitey Witt, chopped one down the third-base line. The ball rolled up third baseman Howard Shanks's hands and hit him in the chest. Witt was lefty all the way and he was across first so fast that the official scorer, Fred Lieb, thought he would have beaten it out anyway and credited Witt with a hit. Ehmke didn't allow another batter to reach base, and Lieb was under pressure to change his decison from hit to error. Even umpire Tom Connally thought it should have been a hit, but umpires cannot make such decisions. Lieb later said, "I had the play on my conscience."

Therefore, Johnny Vander Meer was the first (and only) pitcher ever to pitch two no-hitters in succession, a feat he accomplished in 1938.

In 1923 Boston first baseman George Burns executed an *unassisted* triple play against Cleveland. With men on first and second and nobody out, Burns stabbed a line drive, tagged Rube Lutzke trying to return to first base, and, seeing Riggs Stephenson had already rounded third, Burns raced him to the bag and got there first.

The poor play of the 1923 Red Sox reached its peak late in the season at Yankee Stadium. Babe Ruth lifted a towering fly to center field, not too deep, perhaps three hundred feet from the plate. Young outfielder Dick Reichle circled around under the ball, watched it come down—and the ball plopped a few feet behind him. By then Ruth was almost on third and he had no difficulty beating the throw for an inside-the-park homer.

When the unhappy outfielder returned to the bench, manager Chance remarked, "Pretty smart, Dick. It's late in the season, and I wouldn't want to get hit on the head either."

And, of course, there were any number of fine players the Red Sox let slip away. In the Howard Ehmke deal, the Sox also got a first baseman-outfielder named Babe Herman, who was immediately sold to Brooklyn, where he hit .393 with thirty-five home runs. "Red" Ruffing was sold to the Yankees in 1930 and he became a big winner for Ruppert. Danny MacFayden, another Boston standout who won sixteen games for the sixth-place Sox in 1931, followed Ruffing. Danny didn't do too well with the Yankees, however, journeying to Cincinnati and then to the Boston Braves, where he became a winner for Casey Stengel. Perhaps MacFayden was a Boston boy at heart.

Meanwhile, Bob Quinn, like Frazee, was going broke. He was considering the sale of pitcher Ed Morris to the Yankees for a reported $100,000, but unfortunately, Morris was stabbed to death at a fish fry in his honor. Quinn had suffered through such problems as the destruction by fire of his third-base bleachers in 1926, a disheartening string of Sunday rainouts, a steady stream of managers and the death of his financial backer, Palmer Winslow.

By the start of the 1933 spring training season, Quinn was almost bankrupt. He had to borrow on his life insurance in order to pay for the food his players ate. It was the depths of the Depression and for Quinn there was no tomorrow. He just had to get out, to somehow repay the $350,000 he owed.

A buyer was found. His name was Thomas Austin Yawkey. Quinn told friends, "I was broke and out of a job, but I was free. I actually breathed a sigh of relief when it was over."

Yawkey would try to change things, and eventually he did. But it remained for Ernie Shore to put things in proper perspective.

"They talk about the Yankee dynasty," Shore said, "but I still think of it as the Red Sox dynasty in Yankee uniforms."

Chapter VII

"I DON'T intend to mess around with a loser."

Those were among the first words uttered by Tom Yawkey, the new owner of the Boston Red Sox. Undoubtedly the fans took heart, because, at long last, here was a man who had a tremendous amount of money and didn't have to sell baseball players to meet a payroll or mortgage payment.

Money? Oh, yes, Tom Yawkey had plenty of that. This was a time in the Great Depression when hot dogs sold for a nickel, potatoes were a penny a pound, a postage stamp cost two cents and nice apartments in Boston went begging at fifty dollars a month. When he came of age, Tom received a $500,000 trust fund. Tom was the adopted son and nephew of Bill Yawkey, who once owned the Detroit Tigers, which was how Tom had gotten his great love for baseball. So Bill Yawkey left Tom $3,408,650 in his will, and Tom's mother (Bill's sister) left Tom an additional four million dollars. Such sums, however, were only part of Tom Yawkey's fortune. From his grandfather came holdings in lumber and ore.

Tom Yawkey had attended Irving School at Tarrytown, New York, the same prep school attended by Hall-of-Fame second baseman Eddie Collins, Tom's idol. Tom didn't really know Collins at all, but they met at the funeral of the school principal. Collins was then a coach and assistant to Connie Mack, whom he regarded as father, guardian angel, mentor and the greatest man baseball had ever produced (few will argue on that score). It was rumored that Collins would manage the Athletics when Mack retired.

After the funeral, Yawkey asked Collins if he would accept the positions of vice-president and general manager of the Red Sox if he bought the team. It was a soul-searching decision, and Collins could do nothing but report the offer to Mack.

"Eddie," Mack said with a twinkle in his eyes, "if you don't take that job, I'll fire you anyway." It was a remark typical of the man referred to as "the Grand Old Man of Baseball."

Yawkey and Collins embarked upon an ambitious plan to get the Red Sox out of the cellar and into respectability. It took money, but Yawkey opened his wallet and Collins dipped in. The Sox traded with St. Louis and came up with catcher Rick Ferrell and pitcher Lloyd Brown, in exchange for catcher Merv Shea and fifty thousand dollars. In a reversal, Collins got George Pipgras from the Yankees, but Pipgras was then nearing the end of the trail. Also from the Yanks came Billy Werber, a former Duke University flash, who never hesitated to speak his mind and therefore did not fit into the Yankee mold. Both players cost a total of $100,000.

The 1933 Red Sox climbed into seventh place, but it was far better than the standings indicated, for they finished twenty-two and a half games ahead of the previous year's pace. The crowds began to sift back into Fenway. At least Yawkey had made a start.

Along the way Yawkey gave the Red Sox fans reason to cheer, although he had to pay plenty for the fun. Having paid off a number of debts, Yawkey was also faced with the mortgage payment to Colonel Ruppert, and he asked for an extension into the following year. Ruppert agreed and expressed delight at Yawkey's arrival as a club owner. Then the Yankees came into Fenway and were beaten in five straight games. The next morning Ruppert's lawyer called and demanded payment anyway. He didn't like to lose that many games in a row, especially to Boston.

"I sent the SOB a check," Yawkey grinned.

With the end of the 1933 season Yawkey began to spend money as if there were no end to his fortune. Part of the cash outflow was through accident, much of the rest by design. The accidental money was shelled out because of a four-alarm fire that destroyed the center-field bleachers. Rather than put up more wooden stands, Yawkey, at a cost of $750,000, ordered steel and concrete seating, with a new right-field pavilion, a new third-base area, and in time, the removal of the left-field embankment, a higher left-field wall with a big screen on top and, in 1940, after Ted Williams had hit thirty-one home runs as a rookie, bullpens in front of the bleachers in right and right center, an area that became known as "Williamsburgh." In fact, Yawkey spent a long time refining the ball park.

Then Yawkey hired Bucky Harris as manager over the protests of Eddie Collins. In that case it was definitely a clash of personalities. Both had been second basemen and battled through many arguments on the field. They respected each other as baseball men but disliked each other nonetheless. As club owner, Yawkey had his way.

Yawkey then exercised his check-writing hand by buying whatever established stars were available for sale. He gave Connie Mack a couple of ordinary players and a check for $125,000 in return for pitchers Robert Moses (Lefty) Grove and Rube Walberg and second baseman Max Bishop. Both pitchers and the infielder were getting along in years, but Collins thought they might have a couple of good years left, and besides, neither he nor Yawkey wanted to waste time nurturing "promising" young players. Red Sox fans were entitled to a winning club.

Other acquisitions during the season included shortstop Lyn Lary from the Yankees, lefthander Fritz Ostermueller from the Cardinals' farm system and pitcher Wes Ferrell from the Indians. Wes, the firebrand, and Rick, his easygoing catcher, comprised one of the very few brother batteries in the big leagues. Another addition was Herb Pennock, then in his twenty-second year in the majors. Herb later became a minor-league coach and Red Sox farm director before taking a position as vice-president of the Phillies.

When the flood of money had been halted, sportswriters began to call the Boston club "the Gold Sox," since it was no secret that Yawkey was trying to buy a contending team rather than develop one. And to some extent those tactics worked, but not as well as Yawkey had hoped. The Red Sox did climb into the first division for the first time in sixteen years, and they played .500 baseball, but there were many frustrations along the way.

Max Bishop was only a part-time player. Walberg, who had been a big winner for the Athletics in 1931 with twenty wins, and seventeen in 1932, was a bitter disappointment as he won but six games, losing seven. The biggest disappointment was Lefty Grove. Back in 1931 the immortal southpaw had been 31-4 with two World Series wins, but for the first time in his great career he was plagued with a sore arm. The blazing fastball was only a memory, the high, hard hummer that had stood the greatest sluggers in history on their collective ears. In 1930, he had won four games in six days. On one occasion, he struck out Babe Ruth, Lou Gehrig and Bob Meusel on nine pitched balls, and another time he needed ten pitches to strike out Ruth, Gehrig and Tony Lazzeri.

Now Grove found himself trying to win with an assortment of junk. He learned to throw a forkball, developed his curve and sharpened his control, enabling him to go 8-8 that year with a monstrous 6.52 ERA. Connie Mack, ever the gentleman, wrote to Yawkey: "We believed you were getting a sound pitcher. Under the circumstances, the Athletics will be glad to take Grove back and refund your money."

Yawkey, also the gentleman, responded: "We made the deal in good faith. It is not your fault that Grove developed a sore arm. The Boston club is willing to go through with the deal."

Grove rebounded strongly after the dismal 1934 season, and came through with a fine 20-12 season in 1935, following with records of 17-12, 17-9, 14-4 and 15-4, posting his three-hundredth victory in 1941.

Yawkey continued to issue checks in large amounts in preparation for 1935. He asked Collins if there was anyone who had the leadership qualities of a Mickey Cochrane, and Collins replied, "The only man I know of is Joe Cronin at Washington. But I doubt that Clark Griffith will let him go."

Indeed, Cronin, in addition to playing shortstop and managing the Senators, was also Griffith's son-in-law, having married his niece and adopted daughter, Mildred Robertson.

At the winter meetings Yawkey asked Griffith bluntly what

he wanted for Cronin. "I wouldn't trade Joe," Griffith said. "I'd want too much money for him anyway."

"Write your figure on the back of this envelope," Yawkey countered. Griffith wrote "$250,000." "Okay, that's it," Yawkey nodded. He threw in Lyn Lary so that the Senators would have a shortstop after the swap. Only the payment for Ruth and the mortgage on Fenway had exceeded that price.

The Griffith sale brought a flood of editorial comment from the sports press of America. One baseball writer termed him "a baseball Simon Legree," but another scribe commented drolly, "Maybe old Griff has something. I wish I could sell my son-in-law for $250,000. Anybody interested?"

Joe Cronin was born in San Francisco on Columbus Day, 1906, the son of Irish-born parents who were just then digging themselves out of the great earthquake and fire of that year. A slim kid in his youth, but well built and finely coordinated, Joe was as good a tennis player as he was a ballplayer. But baseball was his number-one sport, and he was good. He was picked up early by a Pittsburgh scout and was farmed out to Johnstown, Pennsylvania, and New Haven.

Pittsburgh then had one of the National League's greatest shortstops in Glenn Wright, and though Cronin showed great promise when he played briefly for the Pirates in 1926 and 1927, Barney Dreyfuss, the Pittsburgh owner, didn't realize what a prize he had on his hands, and Donie Bush, the Pirates' manager, didn't think Cronin could hit big-league pitching. So Joe was sold to Kansas City in 1928. Cronin was there only half a season, when he was traded to Washington.

Joe's progress from then on was meteoric. In 1930, his second complete season with Washington, he hit .346 and played such a dazzling brand of shortstop that he was voted the American League's most valuable player. There had been a tendency to belittle Joe's shortstop play, but the writers of his day gave him full acclaim. He won the shortstop position on the *Sporting News* annual All-Star team in 1930, 1931, 1932, 1933, 1934, 1938 and 1939 and played short for the American League in all the All-Star squads from 1933 to 1941, inclusive, with the exception of 1940.

And still Yawkey kept his wallet open. From the Yankees

he purchased an outfielder named Dusty Cooke and pitcher Henry Johnson. All these acquisitions did little good. The Sox did not have consistent pitching, a problem that was to plague the club for years to come.

Among the characters Cronin brought with him to Boston were Al Schacht and Moe Berg. There are more baseball stories about these two gentlemen than perhaps any others in the game. As a player, neither was more than average, but as personalities they were among the most delightful people in any profession.

Schacht was a pitcher of sorts, with a fund of gags and stories that seemed inexhaustible. When his playing days were over he became a magnificent clown, drawing almost as many fans as any superstars. His "act" was hilarious. Schacht would strut onto the field wearing a battered top hat, a cutaway coat inches too short and baseball pants. He would bring an imaginary ball to the mound and then, in pantomime, go through the wildest gyrations imaginable. He got into mock arguments with umpires, who good-naturedly went along with the fun. His windup and stretch positions and his slow-motion movements were crazy, and the climax of a bases-loaded home run off his phantom delivery was a classic in itself. He would slouch mournfully back to the dugout, then appear moments later as his old sprightly self and bow to the cheers and applause of the fans.

Moe Berg was a second-string catcher and a first-class linguist. He was a Phi Beta Kappa from Princeton, a Rhodes Scholar and a qualified attorney, and at the time he joined the Red Sox he could speak half a dozen languages fluently and was able to make himself understood in several others. On a trip to the Orient he learned Japanese in less than two months. On several trips to Japan, Berg, who had secretly joined General Bill Donovan's Office of Strategic Services (OSS), reported the Japanese secretive plans to rebuild the armed forces of the country prior to World War II. He was a strange but heroic figure, and served his country with distinction.

At one time the Sox had four players who had grown up speaking languages other than English: Mel Almada spoke Spanish, Fabian Gaffke spoke German, Gene Desautels spoke

French and Dom Dallessandro spoke Italian. Each also knew a smattering of another language, so, just to pass the time, Berg engaged all of them in conversation, and while their teammates stared bug-eyed, the five baseball players spent an entire road trip speaking everything but English.

Cronin's managerial skills could bring the Sox a gain of only one and a half games over the previous season. Only Grove and Ferrell were good pitchers; the rest sputtered all year long. Between them the two aces of the staff won forty-five games, accounting for more than half the Boston victories.

One of Boston's losses that season came about on a fluke play that has never been duplicated, probably because chances of it happening again are almost nil. The Sox were trailing Cleveland, 5–1, but they loaded the bases with nobody out in the ninth inning. Cronin came to bat and sent a screaming liner down the third-base line, ticketed for a sure double. The ball hit Odell "Bad News" Hale, the Cleveland third baseman, smack on the head, then it caromed over to shortstop where Knickerbocker caught it on the fly and tossed it to second. The relay to first nipped that runner for one of the most unusual triple plays ever seen.

Yawkey was no quitter. Just as Ruppert had raided Frazee's Red Sox, so did the Boston owner strip Connie Mack of his remaining stars. For $150,000 Yawkey purchased Jimmy Foxx and pitcher John Marcum. In addition, Roger "Doc" Cramer, a good outfielder, infielder Eric McNair and several others were tossed in for additional cash.

Foxx was a murderous hitter. In 1932 he had hit fifty-eight home runs; he won two Triple Crowns and was chosen MVP twice. Foxx could catch, play first and third base and, although no fancy Dan, he got the job done.

Pitchers dreaded the sight of Foxx as he dug in at the plate, flexing his powerful, hairy arms, glaring menacingly toward the mound. Once Lefty Gomez, the peerless Yankee lefthander, kept shaking off catcher Bill Dickey's signs until there was nothing left to signal for. Sighing, Dickey took off his mask and ambled out to Gomez.

"Okay," he said quietly, "you tell me, how do you want to pitch to Foxx?"

Lefty scuffed his toe in the dirt, looked up and replied, "To tell you the truth, Bill, I'd rather not pitch to him at all."

In the six years Foxx played with Boston, he averaged thirty-five home runs. He set the Red Sox mark with fifty in 1938, a year he also drove in 175 runs, totalled 398 bases, batted .349 and won his third MVP award. At one time he was walked on six successive trips to the plate by St. Louis pitchers. Twice he cleared the roof in Chicago's Comiskey Park. When he ended his career with the Phillies, he had hit 534 home runs, which was then second only to Babe Ruth's 714.

Ted Williams said of Foxx, "Next to Joe DiMaggio, Foxx was the greatest player I ever saw. I truly admired him. He was such a good-natured guy, a big farm boy from Maryland. He never bad-mouthed anyone. What a disposition, always a giggle. He never made any bones about his love for scotch. He used to say he could drink fifteen of those little miniature bottles and not be affected."

Unfortunately, baseball was the only profession at which Foxx could make a living. He invested in a Florida golf course and an Illinois restaurant, he tried broadcasting baseball in Boston, and at one time he drove a gasoline truck, but had to stop because of a heart condition. To the very end he never lost his affable disposition.

"I earned $175,000 playing baseball," Foxx said in 1950, "and didn't have a dime to show for twenty years in the game. I don't feel badly for myself. The money I lost and blew was my own fault. I had to wonder if I wasn't born to be broke."

In 1957, at the age of sixty, Jimmy Foxx choked to death on a chicken bone.

That the Red Sox could not win a pennant during those years was only partly Cronin's fault. Some experts said he was too lenient, others claimed he bore down too hard. He hated to chastise his players because he was one of them, but he also realized that he was the team's manager, a job he didn't relish after a while. Individually, several players had great years, but they just never jelled as a unit. For instance:

In 1934, Wes Ferrell was 14–5, then won twenty-five and twenty games his next two seasons. But he was somewhat unique. Ferrell was a firm believer in astrology, and when his astral signs were bad on a given day, trainer Win Green warned everyone in the clubhouse to be careful what they said or did. In 1934, when Foxx was still with the Athletics, Ferrell was coasting with a 10–1 lead and gave up a grand slam to his future teammate. After the inning, Ferrell came back to the dugout and punched himself on the jaw with a right uppercut, then he hit his head against the wall, rolled over and hit himself with a left hook. He kept hitting himself until teammates got him in hand.

In 1936, angry over the slipshod play of his mates, Ferrell threw his cap and glove into the air and stormed out of Yankee Stadium. Cronin promptly fined him a thousand dollars. When he heard about the fine, Ferrell snarled, "I'm going to punch out that dumb Irishman."

Cronin, who was not exactly defenseless, told New York sportswriter John Kiernan, "If he wants to slug me, I'll be passing through the lobby at six o'clock on my way to dinner."

Ferrell didn't show up. But neither did he change his ways. He was a fine pitcher and a dangerous hitter—he hit sixteen home runs, second on the Red Sox pitchers' list to Earl Wilson, who had seventeen—but he was a disruptive influence and had to go.

Never was there such a collection of prima donnas as the Red Sox enrolled through the late 1930s. Without doubt the worst offender was Lefty Grove, whose antics would *never* be tolerated by any modern baseball team—neither the owner nor the players. Manager Joe Cronin had to restrain himself from killing his star southpaw on more than one occasion.

Grove had a terrible temper. He hated all fans, perhaps with some small reason. (He was quoted as saying, "The trouble with fans is they don't leave players alone.") And he could be openly contemptuous of teammates who made errors while he was pitching. Once Eric McNair made a critical error and Grove stood on the mound, chewing his glove in disgust. When the Sox couldn't score for him in Chicago, he sneered, "You think Grove is going to pitch his arm off for you hitless wonders?" At that time he refused to ride on the team bus, preferring to walk the five miles between Comiskey Park and the hotel.

Lefty spared no one, not even his manager. Cronin made an error that lost a game for Grove, and if anyone hated to lose it was Joe Cronin. He had gotten down on one knee to field a grounder, only to have the ball go through him, and after the game Grove screamed at Cronin, in the clubhouse and in Cronin's office. He got up on a chair and said, "You sophomore so-and-so, why don't you field the ball like a man? You couldn't play on my high school team!"

Grove could be nasty, but he wasn't stupid. When he threw a tantrum, he punched walls and lockers with his right hand, not with his pitching paw. Once he told Bill Werber (who also had difficulty controlling himself, as he proved when he broke his toe kicking a water bucket), "Bill, you should kick an empty water bucket, and always kick it with your whole foot, not just your toe."

Outfielder Ben Chapman ranked high in the temper department. He came to the Red Sox in a trade, and his tenure with the club was marked by one escapade after another. Two weeks after he joined the club, Chapman was fined fifty dollars and suspended for three days. He had caught a ball in right field and buzzed a throw to the plate that hit umpire John Quinn. The previous inning Quinn had called Chapman out on strikes and Chapman wasn't too thrilled with the decision.

Chapman was tossed out of another game three days later. Two days after that he got into a brawl with Detroit catcher Ray Hayworth. The following year he engaged in fisticuffs with catcher Birdie Tebbetts. On one occasion he refused to obey the bunt sign, swung away and hit into a double play, which caused Cronin to bench him for ten games.

"I don't bunt," was Chapman's explanation.

Bobo Newsom, who also came in a trade, was an outstanding pitcher with an ego to match. Newsom had a mental block when it came to pitching with his manager playing behind him. Cronin, who had studied the AL players, tried to give his hurler some advice. Bobo responded, "I think I know a little bit about this pitching business myself."

Over the years Newsom, Ferrell and Werber were dealt away, but not Grove. Yes, Lefty was an SOB—wicked, supercilious, a pain to his manager—but how many pitchers have won three hundred games in a career, even among those in the Hall of Fame? Precious few, and "Old Mose" was a legend, a pitcher who, on the free-agent market of this day, would command millions.

Yet, player by player, they did deliver the goods. Grove's and Ferrell's statistics have been cited, but others included Chapman's thirty-five stolen bases in 1937 and his .340 average the following year, Roy Johnson's .300 average in both 1934 and 1935, and Doc Cramer's mighty fine fielding and hitting, which saw him bat .307 in 1937 and .301 in 1938.

That 1938 team was in many respects the equivalent of the Yankees' "Murderers' Row." Every regular hit .300 or better, except for second baseman Bobby Doerr (.289) and catcher Gene Desautels (.291, which is close enough to .300 to merit consideration). "Double-X" Foxx had that fifty-eight home run–175-RBI year, Joe Vosmik, also part of the Red Sox via a trade, had 201 hits and 121 runs, Cronin had fifty-one doubles, and the team as a whole batted .299.

But the pitching—the *pitching!*—was absent. That season Jim Bagby won fifteen and lost eleven, Jack Wilson won fifteen and lost fifteen games. No ball club can win with a staff like that.

Even Tom Yawkey understood that he could not buy a pennant. "Ruppert won some pennants when he was able to reach into the Red Sox for players," he told Eddie Collins. "But it didn't seem to work for us when we tried to buy Connie Mack's old champions. So we've got to try to raise our own. We've got to build up a farm system like Branch Rickey built for Sam Breadon at St. Louis and George Weiss and Ed Barrow built for Ruppert in New York. That's the only way we can catch the Yankees."

Yawkey, of course, was right. Here was a man who had spent millions trying to bring his beloved Boston Red Sox a winning combination, and all his money could not do it. Very seldom did the club break even, let alone make money. Yet in part it was his own fault. He was, to put it bluntly, a good, soft-hearted, charitable, decent, forgiving human being, and he was taken advantage of constantly.

There were things Tom Yawkey was *not*. He was no racist, in spite of the fact that the Red Sox were the last of the sixteen clubs to have a black player. Yawkey merely did things in what was then the *accepted* way, and he was a part of baseball. When the barriers finally fell, he signed blacks as easily as he had signed anyone else; Jim Rice of today's Sox is living proof. Nor did he try to interfere with his players or his managers.

"People would see him sitting around the clubhouse," Carl Yastrzemski said of his boss. "They would think he was somehow undermining all levels of authority, but that wasn't the case at all. He just liked to talk baseball, and that's it."

Thomas Austin Yawkey, a true gentleman all the way, never got to see his beloved Red Sox beat the tar out of the Yankees. He never got to see a world championship team, more's the pity. But he helped bring any number of stars into baseball, and those who knew him best loved him best.

Among them was a tall, lean, splinter of a man who played the outfield for the Boston Red Sox. There are those who say he practically invented hitting.

His name: Ted Williams.

Chapter VIII

IN THE history of baseball, the names of several magnificent players have become forever associated with the names of their ball clubs, particularly during the last half century. Yankee fans point with pride to Joe DiMaggio, Lou Gehrig and Mickey Mantle; Brooklyn Dodger rooters nostalgically recall Jackie Robinson, Peewee Reese, Gil Hodges and Roy Campanella; the Giants of New York and San Francisco have their Willie Mays, the Cincinnati Reds can boast of Johnny Bench. These athletes played their entire careers with one club (in the case of Willie Mays, the final few months with the New York Mets were more for crowd appeal than his vanished ability. He was through by then). The Red Sox had to wait a long time until their authentic hero came down the pike.

Babe Ruth cannot be counted among the stalwarts of the Red Sox. To be sure, he performed marvelously while wearing the crimson hose, but fans saw him display most of his heroic feats while he wore Yankee pinstripes. And Cy Young counts —but that was three-quarters of a century ago, and hardly a man is now alive who saw him at his best. Tris Speaker won a batting title while with the Cleveland Indians, after some outstanding years with the Red Sox.

Therefore, the first superstar who played out his entire career *exclusively* with the Boston Red Sox was a lean, steely-eyed man named Theodore Samuel Williams. After he became a regular in 1939, except when he was injured, it took two wars to get him out of the lineup. Anyone who has ever seen a bat make contact with a baseball will agree without carp or cavil that he was among the half-dozen greatest hitters of all time.

Ted Williams was born on August 30th, 1918, just twelve days before the Armistice ended World War I. His father was an itinerant worker who went from place to place looking for jobs, his mother, the former May Venzer, was part French, part Mexican, worked for the Salvation Army and was known variously as "Salvation May" or "the Sweetheart of San Diego" and Ted grew up an introvert, a loner, who seemed to hear every word whispered about him, words which often offended him and touched off his trigger temper.

When he was sixteen, baseball people began hearing strange things about the skinny left-handed pitcher who played for San Diego's Herbert Hoover High School and batted .430 for three years of varsity ball. His baseball coach at Herbert Hoover High was Wes Caldwell, and Wes said that at times he would follow Ted along on the bases and hit him with a switch when he felt Ted was not running fast enough. Elmer Hill, a fireman who happened to know New York Yankees scout Bill Essick, arranged a meeting with Ted's mother. May Williams asked for a guarantee of a thousand dollars. The Yankees, awash in money, decided not to risk the thousand. With that in mind one must pause to wonder what records Williams might have set had he come to Yankee Stadium with its short right-field fence.

A year later Williams batted .403 for his high school team, which prompted Bill Lane, the owner of the San Diego Padres of the Pacific Coast League, to summon Williams to his ball park for a tryout. While Lane and some other Padres (including young Bobby Doerr) watched with amazement, Teddy slammed pitch after pitch over the wall in right field. Lane sprinted directly to his office to get a pen and a contract.

This was about the time Tom Yawkey had decided to rebuild the Red Sox with young players brought up from the farm system. He had placed Billy Evans, former umpire and Cleveland general manager, in charge of the operation, with Eddie Collins having the final say in the selection of minor-league prospects.

Williams, meanwhile, showed Padres manager Frank Shellenback that he was no pitcher. He had only average speed and his fastball was as straight as a string, with no movement or hop to it. After three innings in relief, Williams was shunted to the outfield, where there was an opening because Chick Shivers, one of the regulars, had decided to quit baseball. So it was during a road trip to Seattle that Eddie Collins first saw Ted Williams in action.

Collins had come to look over a promising second baseman named Bobby Doerr and a young shortstop named George Myatt. He liked the looks of Doerr, but was not overly impressed by Myatt's play. And he also noticed a kid in the outfield who had the finest natural swing he had seen in many years. Later, he had a long conversation with Bill Lane.

"We'll pick up the option on Doerr," Collins said, "but I'm not interested in Myatt. I don't think he can make good in the big leagues."

"You're making a mistake," Lane protested. "A few other clubs are interested in Myatt. Why not keep them together as a combination?"

"Because I've watched Myatt play for two weeks," Collins insisted, "and maybe he can play some other position, but not shortstop. If you shift him, maybe I'll think about him."

Lane wanted Myatt to stay at short. The Red Sox did not pick him up. Later, Myatt did come to the majors but couldn't stick very long. Collins, as usual, was right.

Another acquisition was catcher Gene Desautels, and then Collins inquired about "that tall, skinny kid who has been trying to play the outfield."

"Williams?" Lane was surprised.

"Yeah," Collins nodded. "I like the way he swings a bat."

"He's still a few years away; he's only seventeen years old," Lane pointed out. "He's just out of high school. But if you really like him, you don't have to buy an option. I promise you right now, Williams will never be sold to a big-league team until you've had a chance to get him."

"I don't need anything in writing. Your word's good enough for me," Collins said as they shook hands.

So Doerr did report to the Red Sox the following season,

with results known to all devotees of the game. The great second baseman, Eddie Collins, knew another great second baseman when he saw one. Little Bobby was a dandy player. As for Williams, after batting .271 in his maiden year in pro ball, other clubs began to notice him.

They saw an awkward young outfielder who sometimes got his feet tangled while chasing a fly ball. They saw a kid with a long, loping stride, who seemed to be just jogging, although he covered a lot of ground. They saw an eighteen-year-old lad who swung at any pitch within seeing distance of the plate. But they also saw a steadily improving baseball player.

"From the beginning, Ted's only weakness was his inability to wait for a good pitch," Shellenback said of Ted's early years at San Diego. "He was so anxious to hit that he went after pitches way out of the strike zone. The smart pitchers kept the ball away. But he learned. Williams always could learn. Pretty soon he became more selective and he began to get his share of hits."

Williams's share of hits in 1937 totalled 132 in 138 games, with twenty-three home runs, ninety-eight RBIs and a .291 average. When the winter meetings rolled around again, Lane was besieged by other ball clubs asking about Williams. Detroit was interested as well as the Giants and Casey Stengel, who would be managing the Boston Braves the following year.

Lane stuck to his promise. "Eddie Collins has first call on Williams. I gave him my word—I intend to keep it."

Yet the deal almost fell through!

Tom Yawkey bridled at the idea of buying another player. "We agreed not to buy anybody and develop our own kids," he pointed out. "Yet you ask me to pay $25,000 plus some other players to buy a kid who has yet to hit .300 in the minors. Where's the sense to that?"

"He's no ordinary player," Collins persisted. "I wouldn't ask you to break the rule if I didn't think he'll make good."

Collins and Evans wore Yawkey down. He reluctantly parted with the money and four players for Williams. It was one of the greatest bargains in the history of sports.

There really wasn't room for Williams when he reported for spring training in 1938. The Boston outfield was set, with Joe

Vosmik, Ben Chapman and Doc Cramer. It was also the year Jimmy Foxx would tear the American League apart. Bobby Doerr, Ted's former Padres teammate, teased him about that when Ted arrived.

"So you're the great slugger from the coast," Doerr needled. "Wait until you see Foxx hit."

Ted grinned. "Wait until Foxx sees me hit."

Williams was not the kind of player who could improve by sitting on the bench and watching other players take their cuts. Of course, in later years, he would discuss hitting with almost anybody, including Foxx, Hank Greenberg, Joe DiMaggio and Rogers Hornsby, but at that stage of his development he had to have a bat in his hands, set the strike zone in his mind and learn first hand the hundreds of details that go into the art of swinging a round bat at a round ball and hitting it *squarely*.

In 1938 Williams remained with the Red Sox barely long enough for the proverbial cup of coffee. In his first turn at the batting cage, old Herb Pennock, then a Boston coach, sent over his slow curve which was about all he had left, and Williams whizzed some sizzling line drives into the right-field corner. Joe Cronin was impressed.

"He's quite a prospect for a kid," the manager told reporters. "I like the way he handled a bat. He holds it back there and swings into the ball like it was a whip. He has a great pair of wrists and knows how to use them."

Williams did little hitting that spring training, but he did do a lot of popping off, and for bushers, that was—and still is—a definite no-no. Once Williams tugged at Cronin's sleeve and asked, "Which squad do I play with today, the regulars or the reserves?"

"Why don't you walk over to the bulletin board and find out like everybody else?" Cronin shot back.

"Okay, sport, have it your way," Williams shrugged.

In a short time Williams was on a bus headed for the training site of the Minneapolis Millers. Johnny Orlando, the Red Sox clubhouse boy, walked downtown with Ted to catch the bus. It was a thoughtful gesture Williams never forgot. Orlando liked to recount Williams's final words before they said goodbye.

"Those outfielders—Cramer, Vosmik and Chapman—they

think I'm a pretty fresh kid," Williams said to Orlando. "Well, they've got the laugh on me now. But don't worry, I'll be back here next spring. And before I'm through I'll make more money in one year than those three guys combined. Listen, Johnny, can you loan me $5.00 until I get to the Millers camp?"

Donie Bush was managing Minneapolis that year, and the antics of Ted Williams almost drove him to utter despair. Bush watched in awe as Williams made opposing pitchers cringe. The entire American Association soon found out about this nineteen-year-old, temperamental slugger, who could end a baseball game with one swish of the bat. He led the league in batting with .366, in home runs with forty-three, in RBIs with 142, in runs scored with 130. He smashed 193 hits, which included thirty doubles and nine triples. He also led the league in bases on balls.

Bush was also having heart spasms watching Williams in the field or on the base paths. A tale of woe was related by pitcher Joe Heving, who spent part of the season in the American Association and joined the Red Sox in midseason. Naturally, Heving was asked about the young man in the Minneapolis outfield.

"Williams," Heving declared, "is driving Donie Bush nuts with his fielding and bringing him back to normalcy with his hitting."

Heving related one story of how he was practically handed a victory by the inept fielding of Williams. "First he misjudged a fly ball and then he refused to chase it," Heving said. "He's knocking the cover off the ball and allowing it to scamper all over the outfield."

On another occasion Williams sparked a come-from-behind rally with a double, then began to wander off base as if he hadn't a care in the world. Bush, coaching at third, yelled warning after warning at the base runner.

"You're the winning run," he hollered. "Don't get picked off. Look alive! You're going too far down the line with each pitch!"

Finally, in a fit of pique, Williams shouted back, "I got myself out here, I'll get myself in again." He did, too.

The Williams temper flared on more than one occasion, and

once it very nearly cost him his whole career. With runners on, Williams took his cut and popped up. That has happened to every ballplayer, from Ty Cobb to the lowest busher, but Williams couldn't accept defeat. He returned to the dugout, and in one blaze of rage he smashed his fist against a five-gallon water bottle. The bottle broke under the impact and the splinters cut his wrist. Fortunately, no arteries or ligaments were severed and Williams was out for a relatively short time. The scar has remained on his wrist. Williams always lost his temper, but never swung at breakable objects afterward.

Williams came to Boston to stay in 1939. The sweet stroke was getting sweeter by the season, as he battered big-league pitching for a .327 average, which included thirty-one homers and 145 runs batted in. He also made nineteen errors in the outfield, and his seeming lack of hustle aggravated everyone.

On one occasion, with the bases loaded, Williams lifted a high pop which Philadelphia outfielder Bill Nagel misjudged. The ball fell safely and a pair of runs scored. Williams had jogged down the line and was on first when the ball fell. Had he run it out, he could have made second standing up. Cronin, angry over his lack of hustle, sent in a runner and Williams trotted off the field to a chorus of boos.

"He has to learn to run out everything," Cronin said sternly after the game. "I guess the only way he's going to find out is when I yank him out of a game when he doesn't. If I know Williams, that hurts him more than a fine. He goes crazy when he has to sit on the bench."

The young man from San Diego improved his average, if not his home run and RBI output, in 1940. He hit .344, but his round-trip number fell to twenty-three and the runs batted in to 113, very satisfactory for a kid who beat the so-called "sophomore jinx." The trouble was, Ted was developing "rabbit ears." He seemed to pick up the slightest remark made about him, voices in the stands seemed to be whispering in his ear. The fans got on him when he acted up. They especially relished one forlorn remark made by the kid when he was feeling blue.

Williams had an uncle in Mount Vernon, New York, who was the head of a fire-fighting company. After an encounter with some boo-birds, he was heard to mutter, "Anyway, I'd rather be a fireman."

Jimmy Dykes, a puckish character then managing the Chicago White Sox, thought that was the basis of a fine practical joke. He got some dime store firemen's hats, a chief's hat for himself, and when Ted came to bat he set off a siren as the bench called out, "Fireman, save my child!" Ted thought it was quite funny as gags go.

The 1941 season established Theodore Samuel Williams as the finest hitter in the majors. It was not merely that he batted .406—that's in the records. It was *how* he did it.

Williams broke out in a rash of base hits from the opening bell and kept mauling enemy pitching day after day. By midseason he was batting .405, and the speculation began early on as to whether or not he could maintain that pace. Only seven players had touched the magic .400 mark: Ty Cobb, Rogers Hornsby, Nap Lajoie, Harry Heilmann, George Sisler, "Shoeless" Joe Jackson and Bill Terry. It was the same type of conjecture that filled the sports pages in 1980, when George Brett of the Kansas City Royals flirted with immortality into the final games of the season. Brett didn't make it, Williams did.

During all the hubbub, Williams delivered one of the most dramatic hits in baseball annals. The All-Star game that year was played at Briggs Stadium in Detroit. Williams had already clouted an RBI double when he came to bat in the bottom of the ninth with the National League leading, 5–4. There were two men out, and DiMaggio and Joe Gordon were on base as Williams faced Claude Passeau of the Cubs. Williams stepped into a fastball and drove it against the right-field roof for a three-run homer and a 7–5 victory.

Through August and into September Williams made life miserable for American League pitchers. In the final week he began to show the strain as his average dipped to .399. Joe Cronin offered him a few days of rest. Ted wouldn't hear of it.

"Boss," he said laconically, "either I can hit .400 for a whole season or I can't. I'm going to find out."

It all boiled down to a doubleheader against Philadelphia the last day of the season. Williams singled his first time up and homered the next. That was enough and a lesser man might have called it quits with the .400 safely locked up. Not Ted Williams. He got two more hits in the opener and lost a fifth base hit on a great fielding play.

Still Williams refused to remain on the bench. He was there for the nightcap, with a clean hit his first at-bat and then a savage rising liner that hit a loudspeaker, denting it and knocking it out of position. The ball bounced halfway back to the infield and Williams steamed into second with a double.

He went 6-for-8 in that final doubleheader, becoming the first big-leaguer in eleven years to reach the stratospheric .400 mark. Nobody has made it since. Yet Williams did not win the MVP award, because a chap named Joe DiMaggio hit safely in fifty-six consecutive games and he copped the honors. Well, if Williams had to play second fiddle to anyone, at least it was to one of his peer group. Not since Tris Speaker had there been a center fielder like "Joltin' Joe."

Less than three months later the Japanese bombed Pearl Harbor. The attack was a devastating blow to America, and caused some agonizing soul-searching by Ted Williams.

Since his 1938 season with the Minneapolis Millers, Ted had been returning to Minnesota after each year, for two good reasons. One was the "ten thousand lakes" which Minnesota boasted. The other was an attractive young lady named Doris Soule.

For any freshwater fisherman, Minnesota—as well as such surrounding states as Wisconsin, Michigan and Iowa—is a paradise. There are muskies lurking in the northern lakes, "freshwater tigers" which can grow to forty pounds and more. There are northern pike, first cousins of the muskie, whose teeth can take a man's fingers off. There are leaping black bass, and a million sunfish, crappies and perch. In winter the deer and bear roam the woods. For a hunting and fishing enthusiast like Ted Williams, this was a spot almost too good to be true.

And Miss Doris Soule was a lass whose face and figure enticed a second, third and fourth look from any red-blooded male. Therefore, Williams established Minnesota as his legal residence.

At the time, Ted was classified 3-A due to his mother's dependency. With a war breaking out, numerous young men were being reclassified, and Williams's case came up. He had to make a difficult decision.

Williams had earned eighteen thousand dollars in 1941, a handsome salary at the time but not quite enough to support both himself and his mother. He was due for a raise to thirty thousand in 1942. All he needed was that one year of bigger money to make his mother comfortable, the mother who had supported the family with her hard work while Williams was trying to become a baseball player. Ted was reclassified 1-A. He appealed to the National Selective Service Board and was granted an extension. That was when the hate mail began to pour in.

When Williams reported for spring training in 1942 he told reporters, "Don't blame Mr. Yawkey or Mr. Cronin for what has happened. It was my decision and mine alone. I'm trying to make a few bucks before I go into the service, and this is the only way I know how to do it. I can get by, my mother can't. If the fans want to yell at me, I'll take it."

Some fans booed, some cheered. Williams went about his business as if his rabbit ears had dwindled to normal size. He kept belaboring enemy pitching, and by the end of the season he was alone at the top, the winner of his first Triple Crown, with a .356 average, 137 runs batted in and thirty-six home runs.

By May of the following year, true to his schedule, Williams was in the Marine Corps. The Navy doctor who examined his eyes was astounded, because Williams had an eyesight that showed up once in 100,000 cases. His depth perception was the sharpest the good medic had ever seen. So Williams remained in the service until late 1945, becoming a flying instructor, playing a little baseball now and again, doing whatever was asked of him with absolutely no trace of his usual temperament. The top brass, he was told, frowned on unusual histrionics.

Naturally, serving his country was paramount in Ted Williams's mind, but he *had* to think what his baseball career might have been if war had not interrupted it. In four years he had batted .327, .344, .406 and .356. He was in his middle twenties, the prime of life for an athlete, and he could never retrieve the lost years. Yet he had matured somewhat, which was a form of quid pro quo. Not that he didn't fling a tantrum from time to time, but more and more he was able to control his moods.

If there was any change in his hitting after his discharge, the American League pitchers didn't notice it. From 1946 through 1949 his batting averages were .342, .343, .369 and .343. His home run totals were thirty-eight, thirty-two, twenty-five and forty-three, his RBIs added up to 123, 114, 127 and 159. Along the way there were obstacles to overcome and awards to be won. It was the same old Williams—stubborn, studious and brilliant, older and wiser but still edgy with fans and writers.

In 1946 Lou Boudreau, the manager of the Cleveland Indians, devised the "Boudreau Shift" to cut down on Williams's hitting space. In this alignment, the first baseman played deep, the second baseman played in short right field, the shortstop played almost at second base and the third baseman was at normal shortstop. The outfield was similarly shifted around. If Williams wanted to bunt or merely slap the ball along the third-base line, he was guaranteed at least a single or even a short double, which Boudreau was perfectly willing to concede.

The formation annoyed the hell out of Williams. He would line the ball right at the second baseman or the shortstop and all he had for his trouble was a loud out. Everyone, from Cronin through the writers down to the fans, begged him to bunt or shorten his swing, but Williams maintained his normal swing, which Boudreau counted on. It never entered his mind that a bunt single went into the record book the same way a line shot was entered. His pride was at stake. And he seemed to be vindicated in any number of ways, such as when the Red Sox won the pennant in 1946, and when he won his second Triple Crown in 1947.

Those who had questioned Williams's fielding began to understand that the "Splendid Splinter" was underrated as a glove man. In the first inning of the 1950 All-Star game, Ralph Kiner lashed a Vic Raschi fastball deep into the left-center alley. Williams went back to the wall, made a one-handed grab and crashed against the concrete. It was an expensive catch for he had to have the elbow operated on to remove seven bone chips. Williams was out of action for eighty-seven games and his average fell to .317.

Williams made no effort to avoid the Korean War. Called back to duty, he flew thirty-nine combat missions and was awarded several medals and citations for leadership and bravery. Once his plane was hit and set afire, but he brought it—and himself—home. Captain Ted Williams was thirty-four years old when he rejoined the Red Sox.

Williams played his last game on September 28th, 1960. As he dug in for his final at-bat, every fan, every writer, stood up for the standing ovation that was practically mandatory. It was the finish of a career that had seen him cheered and booed, vilified and lauded, interviewed, discussed, studied, held up as an example of what a modern hitter could do if he had the talent and determination of a Ted Williams. The Thumper did not disappoint anyone. With a 1-and-1 count, Williams sent the baseball into the Red Sox bullpen for his final home run.

It would be an exercise in futility to compare Ted Williams with any other batter. After all, Ruth, Cobb, Aaron and all the rest did not lose the better part of five years in military service; they played in ball parks with friendlier fences than the one Williams had to contend with at Fenway. One sportswriter, however, came up with an interesting observation, comparing Williams with Ty Cobb. When Cobb was forty-two years old, he batted .323 and hit one home run. When Williams was forty-two years old he batted .328 and hit twenty-nine home runs. It's in the record books.

There have been many players who called the Red Sox their home team throughout their careers. Dom DiMaggio was one, Bobby Doerr was another; they and their teammates who wore the crimson stockings and no others have made their marks and could have made any city proud to call them adopted sons. But only two have stood out like beacons in a misty harbor, Hall-of-Fame sure-shots from the moment they began to patrol the outer garden of Fenway. One was Ted Williams. The other, Carl Yastrzemski.

Chapter IX

AS THE 1930s became part of history and the 1940s began, the Red Sox began to look like a contending major-league team, and in good part the younger players showed the way. Bobby Doerr was entrenched at second base and he ranked among the best in both leagues. A young third baseman out of the University of Alabama, Jim Tabor, took the starting job away from Pinky Higgins and stung the ball regularly. On July 4th, 1939, Tabor hit four home runs in a doubleheader against the Athletics, two of them with the bases loaded. Dom DiMaggio—"Joe's little brother"—took up his duties in the Red Sox outfield after three smashing years as the star of the San Francisco Seals, as a replacement for the injured Ted Williams. When Ted returned to the lineup several days later, Dom was shifted to center field because of his speed and his ability to catch balls while on a dead run. That first year—1940—Dom appeared in 108 games and hit for a consistent .301 average. Dubbed "the Little Professor" because of his scholarly, conservative mien, Dom roamed center field for the Sox until 1953, with three years out of the lineup because of his duties in the Armed Forces, from 1943 to 1945.

Although not as big and powerful as brother Joe, Dom was every bit as good in the field. He played a shallow center field, and at the crack of the bat was off, running like the wind. As he caught the ball, he would wheel in his tracks and fire it, in the same motion and with uncanny accuracy, and always to the right base. Dom was not a home-run hitter, but he was a solid line-drive hitter, who delivered in a pinch. And he compiled a .298 average for his eleven years as an active Bosox star.

A strong, hard-hitting Slav named Johnny Pesky became the shortstop, and he remained a fixture at short for ten years. Pesky was a slashing line-drive hitter and could make all the tough plays at shortstop. He had a marvelously strong arm and hit better than .300 every year but one during his years with the Bosox.

As always, the Boston nemesis was the New York Yankees. There seemed to be no way those Yankee devils could lose. In 1938 and 1939, not content with winning the American League pennant, they swept the Cubs and Reds in four straight during the World Series. In 1940 the Sox slipped to fourth, and the impatient Boston fans began to howl for blood, blaming Cronin, Collins, the Boston pitching staff and anyone else who seemed a likely target. Yawkey, they screamed, had wasted his money.

To some extent the fans did have a beef, especially where the pitching was concerned, and 1939 was a case in point. Eldon Auker, a submarine hurler with a wicked curveball who had helped pitch Detroit to pennants in 1934 and 1935, won nine and lost ten, all his victories coming on the road. Denny Galehouse, acquired because he could always beat the Red Sox, couldn't beat many other teams and he too was 9–10. Lefty Grove won fifteen, but he could pitch only on Sunday because his ancient arm required a full week's rest. Fritz Ostermueller won eleven, but he was supposed to do better than that. Young Jim Bagby was an in-and-outer. Hard-working Jack Wilson also won eleven. Only Joe Heving, pitching in relief, turned in dependable work, but the Sox needed starters, not relievers.

If Cronin was to blame, it was because of his playing, not his managing. He was visibly slower at shortstop, but he could still hit a baseball and the only substitute for him seemed to be a kid playing for Louisville. His name was Harold "Peewee" Reese. The Red Sox certainly missed one of baseball's great stars when they let Reese slip away to the Brooklyn Dodgers. In the development of the Red Sox farm system, Yawkey acquired controlling interest in the Louisville Colonels of the American Association for $185,000. "We bought the Louisville club largely to get Peewee Reese, their great shortstop," said Billy Evans, a Sox official. However, Evans and Joe Cronin didn't see eye to eye on Reese, who was sold to the Brooklyn Dodgers in 1940 for a reported $100,000. Cronin personally scouted Reese and thought he was too light for big-league play. "Besides," said Joe, "I think I'm able to play for at least another couple of years."

The Red Sox were in the process of rebuilding, even though the standings didn't always show it. In 1942 the team finished second to the Yankees for the fourth time in five seasons. They skidded to seventh the following year, but that was because Uncle Sam raided the team. Changing uniforms were Ted Williams, Dom DiMaggio, Johnny Pesky, catcher Frankie Pytlak, pitchers Joe Dobson, Charley Wagner and Earl Johnson, and others. The following year Bobby Doerr was in the army. Joe Cronin had to play much more frequently than he wanted to, but if he could no longer make the plays at short, his bat spoke volumes. He hit .312 in fifty-nine games, including a record five home runs as a pinch hitter.

Cronin always was tough in the clutch. On June 17th, 1943, he pinch hit home runs in both ends of a doubleheader against the Athletics. It was astonishing to watch the man. Only two days earlier he had hit a pinch home run, making his total three homers in four at-bats as a pinch hitter. Connie Mack said of him, "Joe Cronin was the best in the clutch. With a man on third and one out, I'd rather have him hitting for me than anybody I've ever seen, and that includes Ty Cobb and the rest of them."

Interestingly, in 1945 there were rumors that the Sox were going to break the color barrier by signing black players. Under the watchful eye of scout Hugh Duffy, Jackie Robinson, Sam Jethroe and Marvin Williams worked out. Duffy thought they looked good and had them fill out questionnaires. They were never signed by the organization.

Robinson said later, "We never thought Boston was sincere. They were just going through the motions."

Jethroe was somewhat more charitable. "The three of us

did well that day," he said. "But the time had not yet come. The time just was not right."

Joe Cronin's version was different. "They weren't ready for the majors yet, but they could play Triple-A. We didn't have a team like Montreal like the Dodgers did. Our top farm club was Louisville. What kind of reception do you think they would have gotten there? We had nowhere to send them."

So the Red Sox were not the first team to have a black player, but rather the last. In 1959, Elijah "Pumpsie" Green came to play the infield, and a short time later he was joined by pitcher Earl Wilson.

In April of 1945 Joe Cronin's playing career was finished. He was thirty-eight years old then, paunchy, and he couldn't even begin to think of playing shortstop, but he could still block a grounder at third base. In a game against the Yankees he caught his spikes rounding second base and fractured his right leg.

The following Sunday a double-header was scheduled against the Athletics, and in the first game, Cronin, managing the game on crutches, started a young G.I. from Shaw, Mississippi, recently discharged from the Army because of an asthma condition. The newcomer's name was David Meadow "Boo" Ferriss, and when he took the mound in his first big league game he was almost too excited to pitch.

His first ten pitches were balls, and he filled the bases with walks in the very first inning. Cronin watched him keenly.

"One more walk and he was out of there," said Joe after the game.

Ferriss settled down and proceeded to pitch a five-hit, 2–0 shutout. He won his own game by slamming out three singles in three trips to the plate, prompting his mound opponent to call out, "Hell, kid, you ought to be in the outfield. You can hit."

One week later, when Boo shut out the Yankees, 7–0, Red Sox fans began to realize a new star had arrived in Boston.

By the end of the season, Boo Ferriss was a New England folk hero. A softspoken man with an easy smile, he won ten games in a row, four by shutouts, and ended the year with a 21–10 record, posting a 2.96 earned-run average. Ferriss had to fight off repeated attacks of asthma but continued to pitch and win.

But for eight straight spring losses by the Red Sox, that year, Dave probably would not have had this early chance in the majors. A former Mississippi State college star, he had little prewar professional experience except as a class B Red Sox farm hand. In 1942 he won seven games and lost seven for Greensboro, North Carolina, in the Piedmont League. Inducted into the Army he served as a corporal, physical instructor, and pitcher for Bib Falk's Air Corps team at Randolph Field. In army games, Boo distinguished himself not only as a pitcher but also as a hitter. With a .417 average, he outhit Enos Slaughter, the Cardinals' star.

Discharged on February 24, 1945, he was orderd by Eddie Collins to join the Louisville Colonels and trained with the team. When the Red Sox got off to their woeful start and were desperate for pitchers, Nemo Leibold, manager of the Colonels, wrote Cronin, saying, "I think this young kid Ferriss can help you." And what help the youngster rendered!

Despite the fact that the 1945 Red Sox floundered in seventh place, Boo Ferriss kept interest alive all season with his great pitching feats. Dave was the first American League freshman to win twenty games since Wes Ferrell did it in 1929, and the first for the Bosox since Hugh Bedient in 1912. Even so, at midseason it looked as if Boo would approach thirty victories. He scored his nineteenth win on August 12, when an asthmatic attack slowed him down. He won his twentieth game on August 26 and didn't get his twenty-first until September 10. Four of his ten defeats were suffered in September.

Boston and all of New England took the near two-hundred-pound Mississippian to its heart. Dave not only was a great pitcher, but everyone voted him a "swell kid." In fact, Jack Maloney, a veteran Boston writer, wrote: "Ferriss had a personality which was infectious; a soft-spoken man with an easy smile, everybody fell in love with the guy. He was brand new. He was a babe-in-arms, but wonderful to talk with. He was frank, but earnest, and braggadocio never had occurred to him."

Despite the seventh place finish, the 1945 Red Sox drew

603,784 at home and much of it was due to Boo; on Sunday, September 23, with nothing at stake, a crowd of 28,743 invaded Fenway Park just to let Ferriss know of Boston's affection for this modest kid from Mississippi. Boo was presented with a new Lincoln, with all the latest gadgets, a gold wrist watch and gold key chain. The Red Sox players gave Boo a radio, and his home town, Shaw, Mississippi, sent a huge floral piece. His mother and sister were up from Shaw and were presented with flowers and other gifts. Then the unsympathetic Yankees defeated Boo, 2 to 1.

Ferriss was one of the few bright spots in the lineup that first year, but even with him, the Sox finished seventh. Like all baseball teams, the Red Sox were marking time until their stars were mustered out of service.

They were back in 1946 and the fans expected great things from their returning veterans. Ted Williams was there, as were Dom DiMaggio, Bobby Doerr, Johnny Pesky, Tex Hughson, Mickey Harris and the others. Joe Cronin was now on the spot. If he couldn't deliver a pennant with that aggregation, his job was in jeopardy.

For the Red Sox, 1946 was a joyous year, a year of triumph, a year of wheeling and dealing. It began when they swapped a pitcher, Vic Johnson, plus cash, for Jim Bagby. It was Bagby's second tour of duty with the Red Sox. He had come up through their farm system, played with them for a time, and then was sent packing when he showed the sullen side of his personality. He was happy to leave Cleveland for a second chance in Boston.

The Sox had long been spoiled by the presence of Jimmy Foxx in the lineup. When he finally wore out there were replacements, to be sure, but none measured up. Harvard graduate Tony Lupien was a good fielder but he couldn't hit, and the Red Sox, who had become gun-shy where pitching was concerned, liked to pile up the runs for the mound staff. Suddenly Detroit decided that Rudy York was expendable. York and Hank Greenberg had been Detroit's fearsome one-two punch for years, and York too was beginning to feel the encroachment of years; his bat had lost some of its potency. The Detroit front office felt that he was over the hill and put him on the trading block. The Red Sox had two shortstops: Johnny Pesky, returned from the wars, and Eddie Lake, a steady if unspectacular player. So it was Lake for York and the Red Sox had their power-hitting first baseman.

The Sox did make one glaring error by selling third baseman Jim Tabor to the Phillies, and that was their weak spot in the infield. That position became wide open when several rookies, including Ernie Andres, Ty Laforest and Ben Steiner, couldn't make the plays, and a revolving door was installed on the left side as one player after another tried to fill the void. Eddie Pellagrini, really a shortstop, was tried out, but he was pressing too hard and failed, although Cronin was loath to take him out because the Sox were on a winning streak. But then, in an extra-inning game, Leon Culberson pinch hit for Pellagrini and got a game-winning hit. Cronin used Culberson at third for a while. Culberson, in turn, was injured when he tried to stop a Joe DiMaggio line drive with his bare hand, and he was replaced by Rip Russell, a utility infielder and pinch hitter. A veteran named Don Gutteridge also filled in. The Sox did not have an established third baseman all season long.

Right field was another question mark. Originally, Cronin had figured George Metkovich to be his regular, but he couldn't hit left-handers, so he platooned with Leon Culberson. But Culberson had a trick knee and couldn't even hit against the right-handers. Cronin, juggling like in a circus act, brought in Johnny Lazor and later Wally Moses, an established player now at the end of the trail, but with some games still left to play. Right field became a day-to-day proposition.

The Red Sox finally—at long, long, bitter last—put together a fine pitching staff. That season, Boo Ferriss won twenty-five, Hughson had twenty wins, Mickey Harris seventeen, Joe Dobson had thirteen. Jim Bagby also made his contribution. During a fifteen-game winning streak he beat Cleveland and Bob Feller, and then took care of the White Sox in handy fashion. The relief corps also solidified. Clem Dreisswerd was called on to put out fires and he responded nobly. So did Earl Johnson.

There were also some fortuitous pickups during the season. The Yankees wanted to dump Bill Zuber so the Red Sox grabbed him, and in his first effort Zuber shut out the Indians. The Pittsburgh Pirates asked for waivers on Bob Klinger and not a single club in the National League wanted him, but the Red Sox did, and he turned out very well indeed. Another acquisition was Mike Higgins for third base, his second chance in a Red Sox uniform. He helped too.

The Red Sox pennant express raced away and by May 10th had won fifteen consecutive games before being stopped by the Yankees. And by the All-Star break they had first place by four games over New York. At Fenway the Sox were practically unbeatable, and by the end of the season had won sixty and lost seventeen in the home park. They were less successful on the road, especially playing at night. Against the Browns under the lights, Boston scored only one run and garnered thirteen hits in twenty-seven innings. But they were so far ahead it didn't seem to matter.

The All-Star game was played at Fenway Park in 1946, and, fittingly enough, the American League roster was loaded with Boston players. In the starting lineup were Ted Williams, Bobby Doerr, Johnny Pesky and Dom DiMaggio. Rudy York and catcher Hal Wagner were substitutes. Pitchers Boo Ferriss and Mickey Harris were on the squad but unused, because the National League got only three hits.

Williams turned the game into his private batting-practice session. He walked his first trip to the plate, and then Charlie Keller of the Yankees blistered one into the right-field seats for a home run. In the fourth, with Kirby Higbe of the Dodgers pitching, Williams deposited one into the right-field stands for his first home run of the game. He had a run-scoring single in the fifth and an infield hit in the seventh.

One of the pitchers for the Nationals that day was a funster named Truett "Rip" Sewell. Back in 1941, Sewell had been accidentally shot in the right foot while hunting, and as a result he had had to alter his pitching motion. During the transition period, Sewell learned to throw his famous "eephus" pitch. It really wasn't a pitch at all but a kind of a weird lob, lifting perhaps fifteen feet into the air with a lot of backspin. As it came down over the plate it looked like a basketball floating lazily downward, and batters almost screwed themselves into the ground swinging at it. Those who managed to get a piece of the ball popped it into the infield. No one had ever hit it solidly.

Before the game Williams asked Sewell, "Rip, are you going to use that stupid pitch in the game?"

"Sure am," Sewell grinned. "You'll see it when you take your turn."

In the eighth, with a pair of runners on base, Williams confronted Sewell. True to his word, the pitcher lobbed his eephus ball; Williams waited on the pitch, swung and fouled it off.

Sewell began to laugh. He threw another lob. Williams let it go for a ball. Then Sewell got cute and slipped a fastball over for strike two. Williams backed out thoughtfully.

Sewell's intent was obvious. He was going to the eephus pitch again, knowing Williams would swing. And wouldn't the Boston belter look silly striking out on that crazy pitch?

But Williams had the answer. As the ball floated plateward, he moved up a couple of steps to the front of the batter's box, then swished the bat around. The right fielder never stirred from his position. It was Williams's second home run of the game.

"I still don't believe it," Sewell muttered when the ball finally bounced in the bullpen. When someone suggested that perhaps Williams was out of the batter's box when he hit the ball, Sewell merely shrugged disgustedly.

"That's the greatest exhibition of hitting I've ever seen," said National League manager Charley Grimm. Williams had gone 4-for-4, with four runs scored and five driven in.

When the Boston lead had reached sixteen games, there was talk of clinching the pennant by Labor Day, but Boston was due to hit a slump and it showed up in September. After Bagby beat Washington 1–0 early in the month, "the magic number" was down to two. Two Red Sox victories, a similar number of Detroit defeats, or one of each by both teams, and the Sox had the flag. They hoped to clinch it in Philadelphia, but the Athletics knocked them off in a short series.

A showdown series with the Tigers was next on the schedule. Cronin gave the ball to Mickey Harris, who fed Dick

Wakefield a home-run pitch in the first inning, and the Tigers eased in with the win. Detroit roughed up Ferriss in the next game and a golden opportunity was wasted. When Bob Feller and the Indians inflicted a sixth straight loss on the Red Sox, the club still did not panic, but there were a few nervous stomachs among the faithful.

On Friday, September 13th, Tex Hughson faced Cleveland's Red Embree. Williams was in a slump; he hadn't hit a homer all month, and when he came up to bat in the first inning he was all the more annoyed when he saw the Boudreau Shift. Practically the entire Cleveland team was in right field. Only Pat Seerey, the lead-footed left fielder, was to the left of center field. Williams decided this foolishness had gone on long enough. He timed an Embree pitch and lofted a high fly down the left-field line.

Even the plodding Seerey would have caught the ball had he been playing in normal position, but it went over his head and rolled to the left-field wall. Williams took off at a full gallop, went around the bases and slid home ahead of the throw. It was his first inside-the-park home run, his thirty-eighth and last of the season.

Embree gave up only one other single during the game, but that run was all Hughson needed. He pitched a masterful three-hitter and emerged with a 1–0 triumph.

Now the Red Sox had a nervous wait while the Tigers played the Yankees. That too was a squeaker, but the Yanks won on Joe DiMaggio's home run, for which brother Dom, Hughson and Doerr sent him a thank-you telegram.

At last, on September 13th, 1946, after twenty-eight years, the Red Sox had won a pennant. At the clubhouse celebration after the game, manager Joe Cronin said, "Now that we've won the pennant on Friday the 13th, I'll never again be superstitious."

Besides the pitchers, numerous other players distinguished themselves that season, so much so that five of the first ten names on the Most Valuable Player list were Red Sox. Williams won the award, with Doerr, Pesky, Dom DiMaggio and Ferriss also garnering votes. Oddly, Williams won no batting titles, due to his September slump. Mickey Vernon of Washington was the leader in average with .353 to Ted's .342. Hank Greenberg had forty-four home runs to Williams's thirty-eight, and 126 RBIs to 123. As for the others, Pesky batted .335, running off eleven consecutive base hits during one stretch. Dom DiMaggio batted .317 and so did Culberson, on limited duty. Roy Partee, the sub catcher, hit .315.

All of New England became infected with pennant fever. Mrs. Mary Cadogan Buckley, the ticket director of Fenway (she was also called "the Duchess"), had to hire a total of sixty-two extra workers to take care of the tidal wave of applications for the precious pasteboards. From the post office came 522,000 pieces of mail containing checks and money orders, while the telegraph service added an additional ten thousand orders. The Sox office was a madhouse as sacks of mail were dumped just about anywhere, and the platoon of clerks and typists tried desperately to maintain some semblance of order. Most of the money had to be returned. Not even two Fenway Parks could have accommodated the eager crowds.

The National League pennant race that year was a dogfight between the St. Louis Cardinals and the Brooklyn Dodgers. Ostensibly, the season was scheduled to end on Sunday, September 29th. The Cards and Dodgers were tied in the morning and still tied in the evening as both clubs lost, necessitating the first playoff in major-league history. For that reason the World Series opener was pushed back to October 6th. The Cardinals won the pennant.

Meanwhile, the Red Sox were in danger of going completely flat because of inactivity. They had ended the season playing lackluster baseball, and the club needed some tuneups which ordinary intrasquad games could not provide. A team of American League players was assembled, including pitchers recommended by Cronin who had given Boston batters the most trouble during the season.

In the fifth inning of the first game, southpaw Mickey Haefner of Washington broke off an inside curve to Williams which went astray. The ball cracked into Williams's right elbow, which almost immediately swelled up. The elbow was numb, and while X-rays indicated no fracture, the pain hampered

Williams throughout the Series. In spite of the injury, the Red Sox were heavily favored to beat the Cardinals.

Tex Hughson opposed left-hander Howie Pollet, a twenty-one-game winner who supposedly had a bad back. If he did, nobody noticed it, because St. Louis was ahead in the ninth inning. Cardinal manager Eddie Dyer, one of the smarter skippers of the era, took a page from Boudreau's book on Williams, except that he exaggerated it to an almost comical degree. Only Marty Marion at shortstop was in an area approaching normalcy. Third baseman Whitey Kurowski played to the right of second base, the rest of the infield backed up and the outfield shifted around too. The "Dyer Shift," coupled with Williams's tender elbow, worked very well for the Cardinals.

The Red Sox were within one strike of losing the first game. Trailing 2–1 in the ninth, with one out, Mike Higgins hit a bouncer at Marty Marion. The ball suddenly stopped bouncing and skidded over the grass through Marion's legs for a cheap single, but the Sox were glad to take it. Pinch hitter Glen Russell singled Higgins to third, but Roy Partee fanned for the second out, bringing up Tom McBride. The count went to 3 and 2, and then McBride chopped one past Kurowski, bringing in the tying run.

Earl Johnson, in relief of Hughson, stopped the Cards in the ninth. The game went into the tenth, the first World Series contest in twenty-two years to go into extra innings. Rudy York broke the tie game with a Herculean wallop into the left-field bleachers, and when Johnson shut down the Cardinals in the home half, the Sox had a 3–2 win.

Boston fans were wondering why Williams didn't take dead aim for that short porch in right field. It was only 310 feet down the line, practically a chip shot for Thumper Ted, and if the high protective screen got in the way of his line drives, the result was still a double. Williams couldn't do it. The elbow hurt like blazes, but he was a competitor from his curly hair to his spiked shoes and he wouldn't give in to the pain, nor say much about it either.

Harry "the Cat" Brecheen, another southpaw, was Dyer's choice for game two, and he pitched an outstanding game to tie the Series. Mickey Harris, the Red Sox pitcher, didn't do badly, but a Higgins error put the game away for St. Louis. With a runner on first and the Cards ahead, 1–0, Brecheen dropped a bunt down the third-base line. Higgins grabbed the ball and promptly threw it into right center, putting runners on second and third. An infield out and an infield hit plated both runners. It was 3–0, Cards.

Boo Ferriss returned the compliment by whitewashing the Cardinals, 4–0, before a sellout crowd at Fenway. Some Boston fans were steaming because they couldn't get tickets. One rooter was so angry that he sent the family's lucky 1826 penny to Eddie Dyer. He had intended to give it to the Red Sox, but since he couldn't get a ticket, the Sox wouldn't get his penny. Ferriss didn't need luck, not with his six-hitter. St. Louis didn't get a runner past second until Stan Musial tripled with two out in the ninth. Ferriss calmly struck out Enos Slaughter to end the game.

The home crowd had watched Williams and wondered. He had astounded everyone and made the headlines by dropping a perfect bunt for a single. It was only his second hit in the three games.

St. Louis erupted against Hughson in the fourth game and pounded out twenty hits en route to a 12–3 drubbing of the Sox. George Munger let the Red Sox hit away because he had all the runs he needed by the third inning. Enos Slaughter, Whitey Kurowski and catcher Joe Garagiola each had four hits, Marty Marion contributed a pair of doubles, and to make the game a totally miserable experience, Bobby Doerr, after hitting a home run, had to leave the game with a terrible migraine headache.

Howie Pollet tried to come back in game five but his bad back kept him out of action. Gutteridge (subbing for Doerr), Pesky and Williams all hit singles and Pollet was out of the game. Williams's hit drove in a run, the only one he would drive in during the Series.

Alpha Brazle replaced Pollet and he did his best, but Boston came up with timely base hits and also cashed in on Brazle's intentional walks. It was Boston, 6–3, and the clubs traveled to St. Louis with the Sox one up on the Cards. Cronin must have felt just fine. Not only had Joe Dobson pitched a fairly good game, but now he had his top three pitchers, Ferriss, Hughson and Harris, rested and able to pitch. Cronin chose Harris.

With Brecheen pitching, the Red Sox had a chance to boot the Cardinal lefty out in the first inning when they loaded the bases with one out, but York killed the rally by grounding into a double play. In the second, Doerr and Higgins opened with singles, but Doerr was out trying for third. The lone tally for Boston came on York's triple and Doerr's fly.

The Cardinals jumped all over Harris in the third with a barrage of five hits to take a 3–0 lead. They got another run in the eighth, and that finished the scoring for the day. St. Louis had tied the series with the 4–1 win. In the locker room Eddie Dyer threw his arms around Brecheen and laughed, "Gee, how I wish you were twins!"

The showdown game saw Murray Dickson facing Ferriss, and for a short time it seemed that the aroused Red Sox would get the chunky little Cardinal pitcher out of there in a hurry. Moses and Pesky opened with base hits, Moses going to third. Dom DiMaggio lifted a long fly, scoring Moses. Williams finally got around on a pitch and sent a long fly to center, which the speeding Terry Moore barely managed to haul in. Only one run had scored, but the Sox were making solid contact with Dickson's pitches.

Ferriss couldn't hold the lead. Kurowski opened the second with a double and scored on an infield out and a fly ball. Four base hits knocked Ferriss out in the fifth, giving the Redbirds a 3–1 lead. Dobson came in and held the Cardinals.

Meanwhile, the straining Red Sox suddenly found Dickson unhittable. Doerr had managed an infield hit in the second, but from then on Boston could put only one runner on base until the eighth, and that was DiMaggio's walk in the sixth. In the eighth, Cronin went to his bench with success. Rip Russell batted for Wagner and singled. Metkovich batted for Dobson and banged a double to left, putting the tying runners in scoring positions with nobody out.

Eddie Dyer walked slowly out to the mound, took the ball away from Dickson and signaled to the bullpen. In walked the hero of yesterday's game, Harry Brecheen.

It was an incredible gamble. Normally Brecheen required

four days of rest, and he was a starter, not a relief pitcher. But Dyer had to go with his best. Brecheen would have all winter to rest.

Brecheen was facing the top of the Boston batting order in Moses, Pesky and DiMaggio. He broke a screwball over the plate and Moses watched it go by for strike three. Pesky hoisted a short fly to Slaughter in right and the runners held. But Dom DiMaggio came through with a solid double off the right field fence, both runners scored and the game was tied at 3–all. It was now Brecheen's game to win or lose.

Williams came to bat with first base open. Brecheen elected to pitch to him and got Ted on a pop-up to second. That was yet another gamble that paid off. Anyone else might have figured that Williams was long overdue to hit one out of the park, for he had sent two long drives to the outfield during the game.

Klinger came in to pitch the eighth for the Red Sox, and Enos "Country" Slaughter greeted him with a single. Kurowski and Rice went out meekly, and then came one of the most discussed plays in World Series history.

After clubbing a double in the top of the inning, DiMaggio pulled a muscle and had to leave the game. He was replaced by Leon Culberson, who was usually an adequate replacement but certainly no DiMaggio defensively. Therefore, when Harry "the Hat" Walker dropped what was essentially a long single into left center, the Cardinals elected to gamble yet again.

Slaughter, the kind of player so dear to St. Louis fans who fondly remembered their old "Gas House Gang" of the 1930s, was up and away with the crack of the bat. He rounded second and steamed toward third under full throttle. Culberson, meanwhile, did not handle the ball quite as cleanly as DiMaggio would have, but he threw to his relay man, Johnny Pesky. It was a decent throw. Pesky hesitated for the barest fraction of a second. Evidently he could not hear the screams of Higgins and Doerr above the roar of the crowd, because as he momentarily held the ball, Slaughter tore around third without breaking stride and headed home. When Pesky looked up he was startled to see Slaughter thundering down the third-base line, and he uncorked a throw that pulled catcher Roy Partee off the bag. Slaughter slid in with the go-ahead run.

The Red Sox came up for their last at-bats with rage in their hearts and determination oozing from every pore. Rudy York opened with a base hit and Doerr singled too, making little Bobby the only player in the 1946 World Series to hit safely in every game. With nobody out it appeared that the Sox had a rally going that could at least tie the game and perhaps even win it.

Higgins bunted too hard trying to advance the runners. Brecheen was off the mound like the cat he was. He picked up the baseball and fired it to second, forcing Doerr. Campbell, running for York, took third on the play.

Brecheen steadied. He induced Partee to foul out to Musial at first, bringing up pinch hitter Tom McBride, whose clutch hit in the bottom of the ninth had tied the first game. McBride banged a hard grounder toward second that took a bad hop and rolled up Schoendienst's arm. There was no chance to get McBride sprinting toward first, and the potential tying run had already crossed the plate. Desperately the redhead managed to locate the ball and execute a backhand flip to Marty Marion as the runner slid in. The umpire gave the "out" sign and the World Series was over.

In retrospect, it was a combination of daring gambles and breaks that gave the St. Louis Cardinals the Championship. Dyer took a chance bringing in the tired Brecheen to pitch in the eighth, but it paid off. Brecheen took a chance pitching to Williams in that inning, but he got away with it. And it was the combination of Slaughter's daring, plus the bad luck when DiMaggio pulled a muscle, that led to the winning run.

Schoendienst said of his momentary bobble on the last out of the game, "That split second seemed a lifetime. I could just as easily have been the goat of the Series."

Third base coach Mike Gonzalez, who watched open-mouthed as Slaughter ran through his stop sign, said in the clubhouse, "My God, I thought he was crazy. Who knows, maybe he is. But who cares?"

In the quiet Red Sox locker room, Cronin was magnanimous in defeat. He told reporters, "We played our best, but it wasn't good enough."

"I blame myself," said the anguished Pesky. "I should have been more alert."

Ted Williams said nothing. He never alibied about his injury. All he could think of were his five singles, including a bunt, in twenty-five at-bats. Williams went into the shower and cried.

It was almost as if some sixth sense told him that, although he would wear the crimson hose for fourteen more years, never again would he have the opportunity to play in a World Series.

Chapter X

THE RED Sox finished third in 1947. Who won in the American League? The Yankees—who else?—aided and abetted by Joe DiMaggio's bat and the left arm of a happy-go-lucky relief pitcher named Joe Page. To be fair to the Yankees —if that's possible—they put on a great World Series show playing against the Brooklyn Dodgers. It was the Series which saw Yankee pitcher Floyd "Bill" Bevans working on a no-hitter going into the ninth inning and leading by a run. Bevans walked outfielder Carl Furillo, and pinch runner Al Gionfriddo stole second. The next hitter was intentionally walked, bringing up pinch hitter "Cookie" Lavagetto, who, with two out, lined a pitch off the right-field wall, scoring both runners. Bevans not only lost his no-hitter, he also lost the game.

As for the Red Sox, 1947 was a time of sadness. The season itself saw the Sox light up Fenway Park for night games, becoming the fourteenth of the sixteen major-league teams to do so. The Red Sox beat the White Sox, 5–3, behind Boo Ferriss.

However, Ferriss didn't win too many more. He, Harris and Hughson all were beset with sore arms; Ferriss won twelve, Hughson had three and Harris had five, for a total of twenty victories. The same trio had accounted for sixty-two wins the previous season.

That year also marked the end of Joe Cronin's tenure as manager of the Red Sox, but he wasn't fired. General manager Eddie Collins was a sick man—he was soon to pass away— and Cronin was tapped to replace him. The new Red Sox manager, coaxed out of retirement, was their old nemesis, Joe McCarthy, who had been skipper of the Yankees through World War II and then had quit because of his own health.

There was some speculation that "Marse Joe" and Ted Williams might not get along. Both had strong personalities, especially McCarthy, who insisted on coats and neckties when the players were under public scrutiny. Williams, who loathed hats and ties, usually came to work in an open-throat sports shirt. Some sportswriters predicted fireworks.

McCarthy snorted over the mere suggestion that he might clash with Williams. He said, "Any manager who can't get along with a .400 hitter is crazy." And he proved it the first day of spring training in 1948 by walking into the clubhouse wearing a sports shirt with no tie.

Most of the Boston players admired and respected McCarthy. Johnny Pesky said, "Joe Cronin was a damn good manager, but Joe McCarthy was the best."

Ted Williams said, "Joe McCarthy was something special. I loved the man. McCarthy got more out of his players than anyone else. He was the complete manager."

Tex Hughson thought differently. He said bluntly, "The only man in baseball I completely disliked was Joe McCarthy."

The unkindest cut of all came with the ballots for MVP of 1947. Joe DiMaggio copped the honors with 202 points, while Williams placed second with 201. Normally, Williams would not have felt ill-used over losing to a star of DiMaggio's magnitude, but it was such a blatant raw deal that he had to make the real story public.

Williams had won the Triple Crown for the second time, batting .343, with thirty-two home runs and 114 RBIs. DiMaggio had batted .315, with twenty home runs and ninety-seven RBIs, a fine season to be sure, but not in Williams's class. One writer had snubbed Williams completely *by not even listing him among the first ten choices!* Even a tenth-place vote would have given Williams two points and enough to beat DiMaggio.

Williams told the press, "The writer's name was Mel Webb. He was a grouchy old guy—a real grump—and we didn't get along. We'd had a big argument early in the year about something he had written." Supposedly, Williams had told Webb he had written "a lot of crap" about him, and Webb was offended.

"I didn't realize until much later that he hadn't even put me on his ballot," Williams continued. "The commissioner should have gotten in on that. The MVP award shouldn't depend on being buddy-buddy with a sportswriter."

In November of 1947 the Red Sox made two trades with the financially strapped St. Louis Browns and came away with some valuable additions to the team. They sent a flock of players to the Browns: infielders Eddie Pellagrini, Sam Dente, Bill Sommers; outfielder Pete Laydon; catchers Roy Partee and Don Palmer; pitchers Jim Wilson, Clem Dreisewerd, Al Widmar and Joe Ostrowski; and, most important of all, $375,000 in cash. In return they received right-handed pitchers Jack Kramer and Ellis Kinder, slugging shortstop Vern Stephens and utility infielder Billy Hitchcock.

The deals seemed to ensure a pennant for Boston in 1948. With the arrival of Stephens, Pesky could be shifted to third base, adding additional power from the left side of the infield. Kramer and Kinder were certain to bolster a pitching staff that had sagged badly the previous year, while Hitchcock was a proven reserve. And indeed it turned out to be an outstanding deal. Stephens, batting with his unorthodox foot-in-the-bucket stance, would average thirty-three home runs over the next three seasons. Kramer was 18–5 in 1948 and Kinder went 10–7. Along with Joe Dobson (16–10) and Mel Parnell (15–8) the staff became solid again.

But the Red Sox started badly. By Memorial Day they were 14–23, eleven and a half games out of first place. Then they began to win and it became a three-team race between Cleveland, New York and Boston, a race which stayed tight until the next-to-last game of the schedule, when the Red Sox had the satisfaction of beating the Yanks to eliminate them mathematically. The season ended in a flat tie between the Indians and Red Sox, bringing about the first playoff in American League history. (Brooklyn and St. Louis had gone through that in 1946, but unlike the National League's best two of three, this was to be a one-game sudden death deal.)

Boston fans were delirious with joy. Since the crosstown

Braves had wrapped up the National League pennant, Beantowners had visions of the first all-Boston World Series. What they did not know until the following day was that Marse Joe McCarthy had been holding strategy meetings with himself. The mental wheels were turning.

McCarthy bypassed his starting rotation and handed the assignment to Denny Galehouse, an in-and-out pitcher throughout his career, with practically nothing left in his arm and only experience to fall back on. Why did he do that? When all the "ifs-ands-or-buts" had been shaken out and examined, there seemed to be as many reasons for the choice of Galehouse as for any other pitcher.

To begin with, a needling Boston columnist said that McCarthy had to go with Galehouse because none of the regular starters wanted to go into a do-or-die situation. That was later angrily refuted by Mel Parnell.

"Pure fiction, a terrible lie," Parnell snorted. "Each of us would have given anything to pitch that game. Besides the honor, it would have meant a lot of money, perhaps five thousand or ten thousand dollars in next year's contract if one of us had been the guy to take the pennant from the Indians."

Parnell had only one day of rest after beating the Yankees. "Gene Bearden, the pitcher Boudreau picked, also had only one day's rest," Parnell pointed out.

Parnell was a left-hander. McCarthy told him before the game, "Sorry, kid, it's not a day for a left-hander. The wind is blowing out toward left. I'm going with a right-hander."

"I thought McCarthy would pick Kramer," was Parnell's response. "But Bearden's a lefty, and he did a damn fine job against us."

Why then did McCarthy go with Galehouse? "I don't know," shrugged Parnell. "Maybe because Denny pitched eight innings of two-hit relief against the Indians a month ago. But with everything riding on one game, it didn't make a lot of sense."

Parnell went on to report that the most surprised man of all was Galehouse himself. He was shagging flies in the outfield when McCarthy broke the news to him. According to Parnell, Galehouse turned pale, took a rest on the rubbing table, then went out to warm up.

"Even Boudreau was surprised," Parnell added. "He thought McCarthy was trying to pull a fast one and had somebody else warming up under the stands."

In the playoff game, both the Indians and Red Sox earned single tallies, Cleveland on Boudreau's home run, the Sox on Pesky's double and Stephens's single. In the fourth, the Indians wrapped up the game with a four-run outburst, primarily because Boudreau used some basic strategy and let the chips fall where they would.

Boudreau let off with a single, and Joe "Flash" Gordon followed with another base hit. Kenny Keltner, Cleveland's third baseman, came up and it looked like the perfect time for a bunt to move both runners into scoring position. But Boudreau knew Keltner was a dangerous hitter and could get the ball into the air if he had to. Boudreau elected to play for the big inning and let Keltner swing away. Kenny responded with a three-run homer, and the season, for all practical purposes, was over. The final score was 8–3. Doerr's homer with Williams on base was wasted.

There was deep gloom in the Red Sox dressing room, but nobody, deep down, could begrudge Gene Bearden his moment of glory. It was the twentieth victory for the rookie southpaw, and he was an authentic hero of World War II. He still had aluminum plates in his head and left leg as a result of his battleship being torpedoed, and he had spent ten days floating around in the Pacific. Never again would he win more than eight games per season in his brief career.

And now, why did the Boston Red Sox blow the 1949 pennant? Two reasons: first, the New York Yankees. Second, an outfielder named Joe DiMaggio, and even Williams said of him, "Joe was the complete player, the best I ever saw in my career." Praise from Caesar indeed! Boston fans may damn the Yankees but, to the last man in the simplest tavern of the city, all have nothing but admiration for Dom DiMaggio's older brother. Few will deny that he was the best center fielder of his time. He could do it all: hit, catch the ball, throw, run the bases. He played with pain, just as Williams did, just as all the great stars did.

By 1949 Joltin' Joe was near the end of his brilliant career. He had limped through the last part of 1948 and had had surgery performed on a heel bone spur. He sat out the first sixty-five games of 1949. The first time he saw action was in an exhibition game against the New York Giants. Joe tested the heel by playing the entire nine innings; he decided that he was ready to play and got back into the Yankee lineup on June 29th, in time for a three-game series at Fenway.

The Yankees were leading the league at the time, but Boston had a four-game winning streak going and the club was primed to close the gap. The presence of DiMaggio didn't bother the Red Sox much. He figured to be rusty taking his cut. Little did they know what the Yankee Clipper had in store for them.

In game one, DiMaggio singled to open the second inning. Two outs later Johnny Lindell walked, and Hank Bauer hit one out for three runs. In the third inning Rizzuto walked, then DiMag saw a fat pitch delivered by Maury McDermott and put it away for a two-run homer. The Yanks won, 5–4. DiMaggio's blow was the game-winner.

In the second game the Red Sox ganged up on Tommy Byrne and Clarence "Cuddles" Marshall to pile up a 7–1 lead. In the fifth inning DiMaggio came to bat with Rizzuto and Henrich on base and unloaded a drive over the Green Monster for a three-run home run. The Yanks kept pecking away, and when DiMag arrived in the eighth the score was tied at 7–all. The Jolter promptly untied it with his second homer of the game. It was 9–7, Yankees, and again DiMaggio had sent across the winning run.

In the series windup, the Yanks were clinging to a 3–2 lead when Snuffy Stirnweiss and Henrich singled. DiMag came up, worked the count to 3 and 2, then jumped on a Mel Parnell offering and boomed a shot that hit the light tower in left field eighty feet above the ground. The Yanks won, 6–3.

For the third time in as many games Joe DiMaggio had driven in the winning run with a four-base clout. His total for the three-game set: nine runs batted in (out of a total of twenty scored by the Yankees), four home runs, one single, five runs scored. When asked how he had managed to do all that after such a long layoff, DiMaggio turned on that shy grin.

"You swing the bat and hit the ball," he said softly.

The Red Sox seemed to have had the starch taken out of

them by the Yankee sweep, because by July 4th they seemed out of it, falling twelve and a half games behind. But Joe McCarthy must have pushed the right buttons because they suddenly turned around and went on a tear, winning fifty-eight of the next seventy-seven, and on September 25th they caught the Yankees. Then they passed their rivals, beating them 7–6 with an eighth-inning rally topped off by Bobby Doerr's squeeze bunt.

Following the Yankee series, the Red Sox went to Washington and returned to Yankee Stadium for a two-game series to wind up the season. One victory was all they needed. They never got it.

The Yanks won the first game, 5–4. In the windup on Sunday they led 5–0 into the ninth. A three-run Red Sox rally fell short, and it was another year the Yankees won the pennant.

Twice Joe McCarthy had come heartbreakingly close to bringing the flag to Boston, hanging in until the final day of both seasons. In June of 1950, with the Red Sox trailing by eight and a half games, he resigned. Steve O'Neill replaced him.

There were several oddities involving the Red Sox during that year. One was a three-game series against the St. Louis Browns. The Sox won the first game, 20–4, and then they followed with another wild score, this time 29–4. In those two "contests," Boston totaled forty-nine runs and fifty-one hits. The third game was won by St. Louis, 12–7.

In a series against Cleveland, Boston made two remarkable comebacks. In one game Bob Feller had a 7–0 lead, but Boston rallied to win, 11–9. The next day the Sox were down by 12–1 and again they surged forward to win, 15–14.

Earlier in the season, however, the Red Sox blew a nine-run lead and lost to the Yankees, 15–10, a game which saw Boston use five pitchers in one inning, equaling a record.

Somehow or other, though, everyone seemed to have forgotten one of the most remarkable Red Sox performers that the 1950 season produced—William Dale Goodman. Billy won the American League batting championship with a mark of .354, a startling figure for a guy who couldn't even win a regular position for himself. The quiet kid from Concord, North

Carolina, barely qualified for the batting title. He needed four hundred times at bat and came up with 424. Yet no one can dispute the fact that he earned it. Baseball has few players in its history who can match the record of this great young star.

At Winecoff High School, Billy was a reversible battery, pitching one day and catching the next. For the Red Sox he played first base, second, shortstop, third base and all three outfield positions.

"I don't care where I play as long as I can play," said Billy. Talking with Goodman was pretty much of a one-way conversation. He was totally unimpressed by himself.

Billy Goodman was no holler guy like Durocher, no fierce hustler like Enos Slaughter. He was kind of a mousey little guy of 150 pounds, a shade under six feet, actually fragile and almost tiny in appearance. He would speak only when spoken to and then not very much. But from 1947 until 1957, Bill Goodman was one of the most valuable but unrecognized members of the Red Sox.

And with Birdie Tebbetts gone, Boston would be weak behind the plate. But maybe this extraordinarily versatile kid would wind up as a catcher.

But for Boston in 1950, the final result was the same. The Yankees won the pennant, with the Red Sox four games out. When the Red Sox finished eleven games behind the Bronx Bombers in 1951, O'Neill was gone and there was a new manager.

Gone too was Bobby Doerr, who retired after fourteen wonderful years because of recurrent back problems. Bobby played in 1,865 games for the Bosox during his fourteen years and compiled a .288 batting average. He was the key to the Red Sox infield and his outstanding defensive ability at second base kept the club together. He was a steady, ofttimes brilliant player, who batted over .300 on three occasions and was sorely missed.

During O'Neill's tenure as manager, the Red Sox had signed Lou Boudreau, Cleveland's former player-manager, to a contract as a player only. When O'Neill was fired after the 1951 season, the managerial assignment was handed to Boudreau. At a press conference after he assumed his new duties, Boudreau drew a gasp from the writers by saying that he would trade any player on the club, even Ted Williams.

Following that announcement, Williams and Boudreau were not exactly on the best of terms. Ted went into the service in April 1952 and returned in 1953, and the coolness between them persisted. There are those who think that Williams decided to play one more season—1954—then retire if he had to play under Boudreau any longer. Williams was back in 1955, Boudreau wasn't.

Boudreau also had his differences with Cronin. The general manager wanted him to use certain players, but Boudreau found one way or another to circumvent Cronin's wishes. Rumors circulated that Boudreau had his eye on Cronin's job, but those in the know understood that Cronin's job was secure.

Boudreau's relationship with the Boston baseball writers was good at first, but as the club slipped in the standings, he became a target, second-guessed unmercifully in print. All in all, Boudreau's three years with the Red Sox were not pleasant.

However, 1952 was enlivened by the appearance of a rookie named Jimmy Piersall, who was to become one of the most controversial figures in all of sports. No one knew then that Piersall was sinking into a mental breakdown, although some of his antics might have given a clue to his condition.

On May 24th, Piersall began trading insults with the Yankees' Billy Martin during practice, and as the words grew hotter, the pair decided to go at it with their fists in one of the tunnels. It took three men to separate them. Piersall went into the clubhouse to change his uniform and then exchanged words with teammate Maury McDermott, and soon they too were punching each other.

A couple of weeks later Piersall got on St. Louis pitcher Satchel Paige, triggering an explosive rally and cavorting outrageously on the base paths. The Red Sox were behind, 9–5, in the ninth inning. Piersall called out to Paige that he was going to bunt his way on and did exactly that.

Then Piersall convulsed the crowd by mimicking Paige's windup, dancing around and shouting "Oink! Oink! Oink!" It wasn't long before Paige lost control of his pitches, allowing an infield hit and a walk to load the bases, while Piersall continued flapping his arms and calling out "Oink! Oink! Oink!" Eventually, Paige forced in another run with a walk, allowed a base hit for a second run and then faced rookie catcher Sammy White. With the bases loaded, White hit a grand slam just inside the foul pole, climaxing his trip around the bases by crawling the last fifteen feet and kissing home plate.

After the game, the St. Louis catcher commented, "That man is plumb crazy. He's nuts altogether. I'll always think so unless somebody can prove otherwise."

Piersall's rejoinder: "I don't care what anybody thinks. We won the game, and that's what counts. Oink! Oink! Oink!"

The following month Piersall was in a sanitarium. Later, he claimed he had no recollection of that crazy ninth inning. Evidently he was suffering terribly. A movie, *Fear Strikes Out*, told the story of the strain he was under.

In June of 1952 the Red Sox and Tigers engineered a multiplayer swap that eventually cost Tiger manager Red Rolfe his job. The Sox sent away shortstop Johnny Pesky, first baseman Walt Dropo, third baseman Fred Hatfield, outfielder Don Lenhardt and pitcher Bill Wight. In return they received third baseman George Kell, outfielder Hoot Evers, shortstop Johnny Lipon and pitcher Dizzy Trout. Strangely, Lenhardt hit a grand-slam home run in his final turn at bat for the Red Sox.

When Tiger owner Spike Briggs was asked if the trade was a good one, he said, "It better be." A month later, with the Tigers sinking fast toward the cellar, Rolfe was fired. But the trade wasn't much better for Boston, as they finished sixth.

The Red Sox rose to fourth place the following year, but they were a full forty-two games out of first place as the Indians beat even the Yankees by eight games. In mid-June, Fenway fans watched a couple of enjoyable games against the Tigers. The Sox won their first encounter, 17–1. In the second encounter the Red Sox scorekeeper needed a computer to keep track of the home team's runs. The final count was 23–3, with the Sox scoring seventeen—count 'em!—runs in the seventh inning on fourteen hits and six walks. It still stands as the modern major-league record for runs scored in a single inning.

At the end of 1953 the Red Sox made a trade that looked as if their glory days might yet return. They swapped pitcher Maury McDermott and outfielder Tom Umphlett for Washington outfielder Jackie Jensen. Boston fans envisioned an outfield of Williams, Piersall and Jensen and were happy with the thought.

It was not to be. Williams reported for spring training, suited up and went to the outfield to shag some flies. Hoot Evers was taking his swings, and sent one out toward Williams, who started in for the ball, stumbled, fell and broke his collar bone. He was out of the lineup until May 16th, but when he returned he was the same old Ted Williams.

In a doubleheader against Detroit, Ted made his comeback memorable by getting eight hits in nine at-bats, with two home runs and seven runs batted in.

In August of that year, Piersall engaged in a throwing contest against Willie Mays in a Red Sox-Giants charity game. On one of his five throws Piersall felt a stab of pain below his right shoulder. He played anyway, and a light drizzle cooled him considerably. When he tried to throw he felt more pain. The next morning he couldn't lift his arm. He could never again throw as well as he could before that throwing contest.

A sixth-place and two fourth-place finishes in three years made Boudreau expendable. The Red Sox had been grooming Pinky Higgins as a manager of the future, and when he guided Yawkey's Louisville Colonels to the championship in the Little World Series, there was no question as to who the next Boston skipper would be. Higgins had been approached by Baltimore and a couple of National League teams, but his heart was in Boston.

In 1954 the Red Sox had signed a kid out of Boston University who they thought was going to be some kind of a superstar. His name was Harry Agganis—they called him "the Golden Greek," and he looked like one too. His parents were poor immigrants. He learned to play baseball and football on the sandlots of Lynn, and he was so good in college that Paul Brown of the Cleveland Browns pro-football team tried to sign Agganis while he was still a junior. Brown tabbed him as the quarterback who would replace the fabled Otto Graham and go on to stardom.

Agganis had a dream—to play baseball at Fenway Park—and Tom Yawkey made his dream come true. The Browns offered him fifty thousand dollars to sign, but Agganis took less money to play baseball and spent a season in Louisville learning what all rookies must know. In 1954 he took the first-base job away from Dick Gernert. Agganis hit eleven home runs—eight in Fenway—but his .251 batting average was a disappointment to him.

At spring training in 1955 he said confidently, "I'm a .300 hitter. I know I can do it." And he began to realize his potential when the season got under way. But he came down with pneumonia and was hospitalized for ten days. Disregarding doctors' orders, he returned to the lineup in time for a western swing by the Red Sox. He played in Chicago, getting a pair of hits on June 2nd, but two days later he complained of fever and chest pains. He was flown back to Boston and hospitalized again. He had a severe pulmonary infection complicated by phlebitis.

On June 27th, 1955, Harry Agganis was dead of a massive pulmonary embolism—a huge blood clot. He was twenty-six years old. Some ten thousand people jammed the church and its grounds for his funeral; more than twenty thousand heartbroken fans lined the route to the cemetery. He was buried on a hillside overlooking Manning Bowl, where he had been an athlete hero as a schoolboy.

The seasons—and the managers—came and went over the following years. Among the skippers were Billy Jurges, Johnny Pesky and interim manger Pete Runnels. It didn't matter. The Red Sox won no pennants, although there were sporadic bright spots which trivia fans could store in their memories to savor on rainy or otherwise bleak days. For instance:

On July 14th, 1956, Mel Parnell pitched a no-hitter against the White Sox in Fenway Park, the first one within those confines in thirty years. It was the first no-hitter by a Red Sox pitcher in thirty-three years, and the first by a left-handed pitcher in Fenway for thirty-nine years. After the game, owner Tom Yawkey tore up his old contract and gave him a new one calling for a raise of five hundred dollars. Shortly after his great no-hitter, Parnell tore a muscle in his pitching arm. He underwent surgery, but the arm was never the same and his ten-year career with the Red Sox was at an end.

In 1957 the Red Sox made a firm offer of one million dollars for lefthander Herb Score of the Cleveland Indians. In two seasons Score had struck out 508 batters, winning sixteen and then twenty games. The offer was reluctantly refused, for the twenty-three-year-old ace seemed on his way to a tremendous career. Two months later Score was hit squarely in the face by a line drive off the bat of the Yankees' Gil McDougald. He never fully recovered. His career as a winner was finished.

Jackie Jensen was one of the finest all-around athletes ever developed at the University of California. He was a fine basketball player, a track man, an All-American fullback for the Golden Bears, a Rose Bowl star in the 1947 battle against Northwestern, a star pitcher and outfielder for California when they won the Collegiate Championship in 1947. He had everything, and when he married Zoe Ann Olsen, the Olympic diving star, it seemed that the Golden Boy had everything in the world.

But Jackie had this dream . . . a dream of playing alongside his idol, Joe DiMaggio, with the New York Yankees, and he wanted it more than anything else.

Jackie was sorely tempted to take a $75,000 bonus from Bing Crosby, one of the owners of the Pirates. Bing had phoned Jackie with the bonus offer and Jackie, although tremendously excited, asked for some time before making a decision. That same day Bing Devine, the top Yankee scout, offered Jackie the same amount of bonus money and without hesitation Jackie signed a contract to play for the Yankees. The Yankee deal stipulated, however, that Jensen play at least one year of minor-league ball with the Oakland Oaks.

Jackie played for the Oaks in 1948 under the leadership of manager Chuck Dressen, one of the smartest baseball men in the game, and Jackie and his teammate, a scrappy second baseman named Billy Martin, led the Oaks to their first pennant in twenty years. At the end of the season it was announced that the Oaks had sold Jackie and Martin to the Yankees . . . for $75,000.

But Jackie's dream of playing alongside DiMaggio was short-lived. He was in and out of the Yankee lineup so often that he never quite adjusted to Casey Stengel's platooning. He was even shipped to Kansas City for forty-two games, then back to New York, and after two wrenching seasons with the Yankees, Jackie was traded to the Washington Senators during the 1952 season. In New York with the Yankees, there had been this great pressure every day to win. With the Senators there was no pressure at all, and Jackie began to hit the long ball and to play regularly.

But he was not happy in Washington, and at the end of the 1953 season had talked to Zoe Ann about quitting baseball. He felt he wanted to be home with his family and he did not appreciate the last-place listlessness of the Senators.

One morning in December, a phone call woke Jackie at eight o'clock.

"Mr. Jackie Jensen?" the operator asked.

"Yes."

"I've got a long distance call for you, sir, from Boston, Massachusetts."

"Jackie?" a man's voice broke in.

"Yes."

"How do you like the trade?"

Jackie shot up in bed. "Who's this?" he asked.

"My name is Hugh Finney. I'm a Boston sportswriter. Didn't you know you've been traded to the Boston Red Sox?"

"I have? Are you positive about this?" Jackie was now shouting into the phone.

"Yes. They closed the deal at one of the meetings this morning. The Senators sent you to the Red Sox for Maurice McDermott and Tom Umphlett."

"How do I like the trade? I love it. Boy, I just love it."

Before the day was over Jackie had a phone call from Lou Boudreau, the Red Sox manager, welcoming him to the club. "We're glad to have you on our side, Jackie," Boudreau said. "That left-field fence is made to order for you. And from now on, you'll be hitting those long drives for us."

In 1954 Jackie played in every one of the 152 games, batted in 117 runs, hit for a solid .276 average and drove out twenty-five home runs. It was the best year he had in his five big-league seasons and he was certain that he would have many more productive Red Sox years. In 1955 Jackie slugged twenty-six home runs, drove in 116 runs and once again played in every one of the Red Sox games. In 1956 Jackie hit for the highest average of his major-league career. He slugged out a .315 batting average, as the Red Sox finished fourth, behind the Yankees, White Sox and the Indians.

By 1957 Jackie Jensen was acknowledged the best all-around player on the Red Sox. Manager Pinky Higgins said it best. "Williams is certainly a better hitter, and Jim Piersall is a better outfielder, but nobody can hit, run and throw like Jensen. He'll be with us for a long time to come."

The 1958 season progressed to a climax exciting only to those fans interested in the tight race for third place. The Yankees had wrapped up the pennant and the White Sox were entrenched in second place. The third spot involved a terrific battle among the Red Sox, the Indians and the Detroit Tigers.

On September 26th, just two days before the end of the year, the Tigers were third, and the Red Sox and Indians, tied for fourth, were half a game behind them. The Red Sox, playing at Fenway against the Senators, had the advantage, since Detroit and Cleveland were tearing at each other. The Red Sox swept a doubleheader with the Senators, while the Indians were beating the Tigers. On the day before the season was over, the Red Sox again trounced Washington, while the Tigers beat Cleveland.

On the last day of the year, the Indians won the rubber game of their series with Detroit, and the Red Sox needed only to beat the Senators once more to clinch third place.

They did it with the help of Jackie Jensen's big bat. Jackie slammed his thirty-fifth home run of the year to beat the Senators, and the Sox finished in third place.

Jensen had had the greatest year of his career. He finished the season with 122 runs batted in, enough to give him title to the runs-batted-in championship. His thirty-five homers left him fifth among the league's sluggers. And his .286 batting average and all-around play earned him the American League's Most Valuable Player award for 1958.

Jackie Jensen was no longer simply the Golden Boy. At long last, he had become one of baseball's outstanding stars, ranking only a shade below the game's greatest.

Early in 1959, Joe Cronin became the first former player to become president of the American League. He was replaced as general manager by Bucky Harris. Oddly enough, when Cronin had come to manage the Red Sox in 1934, he had replaced Bucky Harris at the helm.

In 1960 Ted Williams retired, his last hurrah being a long home run into the right-field seats. Following the clout, he took the field, only to see a grinning Carroll Hardy lope out to replace him, so that Williams could have still another ovation to hear as his career ended.

Later, Williams said, "They reacted like nothing I have ever heard. They cheered like hell . . . and the cheering grew louder and louder. I thought about tipping my hat . . . but I knew I couldn't do it. It just wouldn't have been me."

In 1961 another rookie reported for spring training, a player who would, in time, become as much a legend in Boston as his predecessor, Ted Williams.

The kid's name was Carl Yastrzemski.

Chapter XI

THE RED Sox public relations director, Bill Crowley, took great pains to inform the public exactly how to pronounce the name of their newest rookie. It was *Ya-strem-ski,* as if there were no *z* in the spelling. The public thought it would be a whole lot simpler to call him "Yaz," and that was that.

It would not be quite accurate to say that Yaz was born with a bat in his hands. Indeed, it wasn't until he was eighteen months old that his father bought him a small one, showed him how to hold and swing it, then lobbed a ball patiently while the toddler swished and swooshed, making contact surprisingly often.

For Carl Yastrzemski, born on August 22nd, 1939, boyhood was idyllic. He grew up on a potato farm in Bridgehampton, on Long Island, which is a long, flat hunk of land running from the borough of Queens, New York, into Montauk Point where the Atlantic Ocean comes to meet it. Most of Carl's relatives were farmers. In fact, Long Island could once rival both Maine and Idaho in the production of potatoes, that is until the builders started building whole towns to serve as bedrooms for commuters working in the Big Apple.

Yastrzemski's introduction to more formal baseball was varied. He played Little League, Babe Ruth League and American Legion ball. He also played with a team called the Eagles, which consisted of a few dozen cousins scattered over central and eastern Long Island. They played on Sundays.

Carl was a catcher. He also played a little shortstop now and then.

Yaz was still no ball of fire in high school, although he did make the varsity. But he couldn't hit for distance, not until his father bought a weighted bat and ordered him to keep swinging it. And it worked! The stroke began to develop. Once he hit safely in fifteen consecutive at-bats, and he had one season when he hit .650.

Then it was on to Notre Dame where the Red Sox caught up with him. He was signed during his sophomore year, after turning down a contract bid by the Yankees that called for a bonus of forty thousand dollars. Carl's father insisted that he would sign for $100,000, and when the Red Sox offered that sum, plus his Notre Dame expenses, Carl signed with the Sox. Yaz promised his father that he would eventually get his degree, which he did in 1966 from Merrimack College. Meanwhile, he had to learn his trade down in the minor leagues.

It didn't take long. He hit .377 with Raleigh, then .339 with Minneapolis, and the Red Sox decided he was ready for the big time. In a way the front office was right; in another way they were wrong.

Defensively, the twenty-one-year-old rookie showed good judgment in tracking down fly balls and an amazing arm which was both strong and accurate. In one game he threw out a runner trying to score from second, and barely missed another one on the next play.

An interested spectator was Joe Gordon, then manager of the Athletics. "It's going to be tough scoring from second on that kid," he observed. "I didn't think he could throw like that."

But Yaz couldn't hit. He got his first home run on May 9th, and at the time he was batting just .246. As the days passed, his average dipped, and he was pressing, trying to get his hits by swinging at every pitch. In Yawkey's mind there was only one man who could tutor young Yaz; he called Ted Williams, who was fishing down in Florida. Always anxious to help his old boss, Ted was there the next day. He carefully studied the youngster's swing and after a few days moved Yaz into a new and more comfortable stance at the plate.

Yaz wasn't a pull hitter then. He was spraying his shots to center or left center because of his closed stance. He couldn't get around on the ball in time. Williams worked with him, suggesting a more open stance with his body turned slightly and his feet positioned differently.

With some youngsters, a change in batting style will play havoc with their thinking, so that they won't be able to hit from any stance. Yaz was willing to try anything. He went from .266 in 1961 to .296 in 1962, and then .321 in 1963, the year he won the American League batting championship. It was the fifth time in seven years that a Red Sox player had taken the title. Previous winners over that span were Williams (1957 and 1958), Pete Runnels (1960 and 1962) and now Yaz. His long career was finally in high gear. Now he would go on to become one of Boston's civic treasures.

Aside from Yastrzemski, the Fenway fans always had some player or other to occupy their thoughts. A parade of the outstanding, the average and the inept kept the good folks entertained.

A highlight of the 1962 season was the sensational pitching of big Earl Wilson. Until June 26th it had been "Wild Man" Wilson. On June 27th it became "No Hit" Wilson. The big, hulking, unassuming Wilson became the first black in the history of the American League to pitch a no-hitter, as he fastballed his way to a 2–0 Red Sox win over the Los Angeles Angels at Fenway. The big right-hander gave up four walks. No other Angel reached first base. Only two LA runners got as far as second base. Earl faced just thirty-one batters. Relatively unknown outside of New England, Wilson, a 220-pound, six-foot-four-inch giant, became an instant celebrity after his no-hitter and appeared on a number of the leading television programs. Suddenly his big grin and huge frame were known from coast to coast. Immediately after the no-hitter, Tom Yawkey tore up Wilson's contract and gave him a sizeable salary increase.

For a time the Red Sox had a first baseman named Dick Stuart. Every time he fielded a batted ball it was an adventure. One nameless sportswriter wrote, "Dick Stuart had a sparring session in the first inning with a ground ball. The ball won."

Everyone called him "Dr. Strangeglove," and it was eye-popping to watch him wave feebly as bouncing balls skidded over, under or through his mitt.

Johnny Pesky said it all when he sized up Stuart with these words: "Big Stu was ten years ahead of his time in Boston. He would have been a great designated hitter because he really could hit and had great power. But in the field he was a menace. Nobody could hit well enough to make up for what he cost us in the field. If you took the bat out of Dick's hands, he wasn't even a good semipro player."

A strapping relief pitcher named Dick Radatz came to Boston and brought his blazing fastball with him. Standing six feet six inches tall and weighing 245 pounds, he was promptly nicknamed "the Monster," and indeed he was a formidable sight on the mound. In 1962, as a rookie, he was named the American League's Fireman of the Year, appearing in sixty-two games, posting a 9–6 record with twenty-four saves and a 2.24 ERA. In 1963 he was 15–6 with twenty-five saves and an ERA of 1.97 in sixty-six games. At one point during the season he ran off a string of thirty-three scoreless innings. In 1964 he appeared in seventy-nine games, won sixteen and lost nine, with twenty-nine saves and an ERA of 2.29.

Ralph Houk, who had seen pitchers come and go during his career as a catcher and manager, said, "Dick Radatz is the best relief pitcher I've ever watched." Johnny Pesky, who converted Radatz from a starter to a relief pitcher, said, "God bless Dick Radatz. He's our franchise."

In June of 1966 Radatz was gone from the scene, traded to Cleveland for pitchers Lee Stange and Don McMahon. That live fastball was gone. He remained in the big league for another two and a half years, winning only three games over that span.

On April 18th, 1964, the fans at Fenway got their first look at a brash nineteen-year-old outfielder who hailed from Swampscott, Massachusetts. On the first pitch thrown to him before home fans, Tony Conigliaro hit a long bomb over the left field fence for a home run. From that moment on "Tony C." could do nothing wrong in their eyes.

Tony hit twenty-four home runs as a rookie and thirty-two

the following season, becoming at the age of twenty the youngest player ever to lead the American League in that department.

On August 18th, 1967, an errant pitch by Jack Hamilton of the California Angels hit Conigliaro on the left cheekbone. At the time he was batting .287 with twenty home runs and sixty-seven runs batted in. He was rushed to the hospital, where the doctors found that the cheekbone had been fractured, the jaw dislocated and the retina of his eye damaged.

"I really thought I was going to die," Tony said when he recounted his feelings.

The injury sidelined him for the rest of 1967. He tried to come back in 1968 but had trouble with his vision and had to quit in spring training. In the autumn of 1968 his vision suddenly improved, and he tried again in 1969, but there was no way he could ever regain his old form. With his retirement baseball lost a talented, colorful young player.

In 1967 it all came together for the Red Sox, despite the loss of Conigliaro. It began when Dick Williams, who had managed Boston's farm team at Toronto, was called in as manager of the parent club. He took over a team that had not been at the .500 mark since 1958, when they were 79–75, a team that had not lived up to its potential.

"We'll win more than we'll lose," Williams predicted before the season got under way. He was right, because they did things *his* way. He set the tone almost immediately by removing Yastrzemski as team captain, a job Yaz hadn't wanted in the first place. When asked why, Williams said, "I'm the only chief. All the rest are Indians."

Williams was a martinet, and his no-nonsense attitude irritated his players, but he couldn't have cared less. When the season was over, Williams explained his attitude.

"They had the talent. It was a team that needed shaking up, so I motivated the guys by criticizing them without letup. Even though we won the pennant, I don't think there was a player on the team who liked me by the end of the season. But I noticed that nobody sent back a World Series check."

Looking for a replacement for the injured Conigliaro, the Red Sox received a windfall when they were able to sign Ken

Harrelson as a free agent through the courtesy of Athletics owner Charles O. Finley. "The Hawk" got into an argument with Finley, and when Harrelson refused to back down, Finley just fired him. The Red Sox outbid a lot of other teams and landed him for a $150,000 contract that ran through 1969. With Finley, Harrelson had been earning twelve thousand dollars.

Harrelson didn't help much the rest of the season, nor was he effective in the World Series, but he had a bang-up season the following year.

The 1967 pennant race was peculiar in that four teams were in it until almost the final day, and each of them treated the pennant like a hot potato. The clubs involved were Boston, Chicago, Minnesota and Detroit, and if any of them wanted the top spot they sure didn't show it.

In the last week of the season it appeared that Chicago had the best chance to win. They were scheduled to play a doubleheader against Kansas City and then three games at home against Washington. The White Sox were only a half-game out of first place.

Detroit, trailing front-running Minnesota by one game, had a pair of doubleheaders scheduled against California. Boston, also a game behind the Twins, had to take on Minnesota in a showdown. Therefore, in order to win the pennant, Chicago had to lose three, Detroit two and Minnesota two while Boston couldn't lose at all.

Chicago took some of the suspense out of the air by losing four in a row, three by shutouts. They finished fourth.

Detroit had already won its first game against California and were leading 6–2 in the eighth inning of the second game. A victory would ensure at least a tie. But they blew the lead and the game.

Boston faced the only pitcher they really feared, Jim Kaat, who had won his last seven starts. The Twins were ahead, 1–0, when something popped in Kaat's elbow and he was out of there. The Sox then commenced to nibble away at Minnesota pitching, and in the seventh inning they put the game away on Carl Yastrzemski's three-run blast into the seats.

It was Jim Lonborg for the Sox and Dean Chance for the Twins in the season's finale. Minnesota took a 2–0 lead when

Harmon Killebrew walked and Tony Oliva belted a drive to the left-field wall. Killebrew, who had hesitated rounding third, sprinted for home. Yaz's throw to the plate seemed to be short, so George Scott, the Sox first baseman, cut it off and threw it toward the catcher. The ball sailed almost to the backstop and Killebrew was in. Another run scored later when Yaz let a cheap hit roll through his legs for an error.

In the home sixth Lonborg decided to try bunting his way on base, and dropped one between the mound and third base. Both Chance and Cesar Tovar went for the ball, then pulled an Alfonse-Gaston act before Tovar reached for it and the ball refused to behave. A seeing-eye grounder by Jerry Adair put men on first and second, bringing up Dalton Jones.

Normal strategy dictated a bunt to put both runners in scoring position. But that would bring up Yaz, who would undoubtedly be given a free pass. Besides, Jones wasn't much of a bunter. Still, Williams signaled for a bunt. Jones fouled it off. Williams switched signals and had Jones hit away. Good old Dalton responded by slapping one past the charging Tovar to load the bases. Now Yaz had to be pitched to, and the Sox slugger lined a two-run single to center, tying the game. Harrelson then chopped one to short, a routine double-play ball, except that Yaz had been running with the pitch and was too close to second. Instead of throwing to first, Zoilo Versalles elected to try to catch Jones at the plate, and Jones was already home when the ball arrived. It wasn't even close.

In all the Red Sox scored five runs. The Twins added one in the eighth, but Yaz stopped the rally by fielding Bob Allison's hit into the left-field corner and throwing him out as he tried to stretch the blow into a double.

Boston was now assured of at least a tie in the standings. It was almost eight o'clock in the evening when the Red Sox learned that Detroit had lost its final game against California. Boston had won the pennant.

The last time the Red Sox had been AL champs, they had faced the St. Louis Cardinals in the World Series. Now, twenty-one years later, the same two teams went at it again. The opening matchups pitted Jose Santiago against future Hall-of-Famer Bob Gibson.

For Santiago, the opportunity to open a World Series was both a vindication and a thrill. Only three years earlier he had spent a season with Kansas City without winning a game. The Athletics shipped him back to the minors and, whether by accident or design, neglected to protect their rights to him. The Red Sox bought him from Vancouver, but not until the second half of the 1967 season did he begin to win consistently.

Santiago was in trouble frequently. There were two runners on base when he induced Orlando Cepeda to hit into a double play, and he faced a similar situation in the second, with another double play helping him get out of the inning. In the third inning, Lou Brock got his second hit and Flood doubled him to third. Brock scored on a grounder to first by Roger Maris, then Santiago retired the side without further trouble.

The Sox answered the Cardinal run with one of their own in the bottom of the third. Santiago did it himself, lofting a home run drive into the screen atop the Green Monster. That was all the scoring for Boston, as Gibson pitched a masterful six-hit, ten-strikeout performance. All things considered, Santiago did a fine job. The Cards scored their second and last run in the seventh when Lou Brock got another hit (he had four in the game), stole second again, took third on Curt Flood's groundball single to the right side, and came in when Jerry Adair made a diving stop of a grounder by Maris but couldn't recover in time to stop the run. The Red Sox couldn't answer that score. After Santiago's homer, only two Boston runners reached second base.

Jim Lonborg evened the Series the following day with a dandy one-hitter that sent 35,188 Fenway fans home happy. Lonborg was pleased too, but not quite as happy as the fans.

With two out in the eighth inning, the six-foot-five-inch right-hander had a no-hitter, and he knew it. Up stepped the light-hitting Cardinal second baseman, Julian Javier, who hit a hanging slider to left for a double. It proved to be the Cards' only hit of the game.

"Losing the no-hitter was sheer agony," Lonborg said after the game. "I threw up my hands in front of my face because I didn't want to look, as if seeing somebody in an automobile accident. I really wanted that no-hitter, and suddenly it was gone."

Yastrzemski, who had gone hitless in the first game, provided Lonborg with all the offense that was necessary. He had a solo homer in the fourth and a three-run home-run blast in the seventh, giving Lonborg a five-run cushion. The other tally was scored on Rico Petrocelli's sacrifice fly that drove in Scott in the sixth.

The teams journeyed to St. Louis where Gary Bell opposed Nelson Briles. Bell was a pickup from the Indians in June, where he had had a 1–4 record and Cleveland had released him. With the Red Sox he was 12–8 for the remainder of the season. Briles had a 14–5 record with a nice 2.44 ERA. Bell lasted two innings and left for a pinch hitter in the third, having given up three runs. The Cardinals added single runs in the sixth and eighth for a total of five. The Red Sox scored only two, one each in the sixth and seventh, the runs being driven in by Dalton Jones and Reggie Smith.

The opening pitchers were rematched for the fourth game, and the result was the same except that Santiago didn't survive the first inning. Brock opened the home half of the first by beating out a hit to third. Santiago tried to keep Brock close to the bag, making three throws to first, but it was academic anyway, because Curt Flood singled to left. Maris lined an opposite-field double to left, scoring both speed merchants. When Cepeda flied to medium-right field, Maris alertly tagged up and sprinted to third, scoring a moment later when catcher Tim McCarver singled through the drawn-in infield. Santiago got Mike Shannon on a pop-up to Petrocelli. The onslaught continued with Javier's infield hit and Dal Maxvill's single to left, scoring McCarver. Santiago was taken out of the box and Gary Bell, who had worked a couple of innings the previous day, came in to retire pitcher Bob Gibson.

With four runs in his pocket, Gibson pitched his heart out. After the third inning he had a six-run lead, and he scattered five hits for a nifty shutout. He struck out six.

Now it was up to Lonborg to keep the Red Sox in the Series and he was equal to the task. Javier singled behind second base in the third inning and Maris hit to right in the fourth;

Lonborg carried that two-hitter into the dramatic ninth inning, clinging to a one-run lead provided by Joe Foy's single, an error by third baseman Mike Shannon and a ground single through shortstop by Ken Harrelson. It was an unearned run. A twenty-two-year-old lefty named Steve Carlton wasn't easy to hit. He allowed only three safeties in his six innings of work.

Ray Washburn relieved Carlton and shut the Sox out during his two innings, and Ron Willis came in to pitch the ninth for St. Louis. He promptly loaded the bases on two walks sandwiched around Reggie Smith's double. When Willis pitched ball one to the veteran Elston Howard, he was taken out. Jack Lamabe, a former New York Met, took the mound.

Howard popped a looping fly behind first that fell in front of the charging Maris. The right fielder picked up the ball on one bounce and fired home, but as he threw he slipped, and the throw was high. Two runs scored and the Sox led, 3–0. Lamabe struck out Lonborg and then Foy. Howard and Petrocelli tried to engineer a double steal on the Foy strikeout, but the Cards worked the cutoff play to perfection. Javier threw home, Petrocelli was caught in a rundown and tagged out.

In the bottom of the ninth, Lonborg got Brock and Flood, surrendered a home run to Maris, then induced Cepeda to ground out, third to first. The home run by Maris was the only run the Cards had scored on Lonborg in eighteen innings, which duplicated Bob Gibson's fine effort.

Dick Williams chose a rookie named Gary Waslewski to pitch the sixth game. Waslewski, a Meriden, Connecticut, youngster, had shuttled back and forth between Toronto and Boston during the season and his selection was strictly a gamble on Williams's part.

Before the game the Red Sox manager said to his pitcher, "Just throw the ball as hard as you can for as long as you can." He was hoping to get perhaps six good innings, and then he would go to the bullpen. That was exactly what Waslewski delivered.

The kid retired the Cards in the first two innings and had a one-run lead on Petrocelli's drive into the friendly Green Monster, but he couldn't hold it. The Cardinals scored twice in the third on Javier's double and Brock's single. Then Brock stole second base and Curt Flood singled to right. The Sox gave Waslewski the lead once more in the fourth on home runs by Yaz, Smith and Petrocelli's second round-tripper of the day.

Waslewski simply was tired in the sixth. He walked Maris, got Cepeda out on a fly, walked McCarver and delivered ball one to Shannon. Williams walked to the mound, patted the kid on the shoulder and took the ball away. In came Wyatt, who managed to get through the inning without damage.

Wyatt wasn't that good in the seventh. He walked pinch hitter Bobby Tolan, and then Lou Brock, who had once hit a home run into the center-field bleachers at the Polo Grounds, smashed a 450-foot drive halfway up the right-center bleachers, tying the game.

The Red Sox did what they had to in the bottom of the inning. Dalton Jones singled, Joe Foy bashed a triple, Mike Andrews singled through the infield, Yaz singled to right, Scott and Smith got base hits, and the result was four runs.

Gary Bell came in for the Sox and he barely escaped with his life. He allowed an infield hit by Cepeda, then watched Yaz make a circus catch against the wall on McCarver's drive. Shannon doubled and Javier lined a bullet that stuck in Joe Foy's glove at third. Maxvill walked, filling the bases, but pinch hitter Dave Ricketts slugged Bell's first pitch right to Yastrzemski for the third out.

In the top of the ninth Lou Brock belted what looked like another home run, but George Thomas, playing right field, hauled it in at the fence in front of the bullpen. Flood grounded out, Maris looped a hit to left, Cepeda grounded out and the Red Sox had tied the series at 3–all with an 8–4 win.

There was no question as to who would pitch the deciding game. It had to be Lonborg, with two days rest, against Gibson, who had had one day more of ease. It was evident soon enough that Lonborg just didn't have it.

Big Jim got through the first two innings but yielded a pair of runs in the third on Maxvill's triple, hits by Flood and Maris and his own wild pitch. He got the third out by making Orlando Cepeda bounce out. It was partly due to Cepeda's bat that the Cards got into the Series, but he was a complete bust in the Championship games. He got just three hits in twenty-nine trips to the plate for a .103 average. There were a total of twenty men on base for him to drive in, but he scored only one.

Lonborg was fading fast but tried to hang in. He couldn't. In the fifth Gibson homered and Brock singled, stole two bases and came in on a fly by Maris. In the sixth McCarver doubled and went to third on Foy's boot of Shannon's shot, and both rode home on Javier's home run into the screen. The score was 7-1 by then, and although the Sox added another tally in the eighth, it was really all over after Javier's crusher. Bob Gibson posted his third Series victory, and the 1967 baseball season was over.

It had been a tremendously successful year for Carl Yastrzemski. He captured the Triple Crown by batting .326, hitting forty-four home runs and driving in 121 runs. He also batted .400 in the World Series.

It wasn't too bad for Jim Lonborg, either. He won twenty-two games that season and received the Cy Young Award. But it all turned sour for him that winter when he tore two ligaments in his left knee while skiing at Lake Tahoe. He was never the same pitcher after that. He was 6-10 in 1968 and 27-29 over the next four years. He spent some time in the minors during that stretch and was finally traded to Milwaukee, and then to the Phillies.

Manager Dick Williams, visibly upset by Lonborg's accident, tried to shrug it off by saying, "Well, I guess you can go out on a golf course and get hit on the head by a ball."

Chapter XII

AS USUAL, the Red Sox couldn't repeat in 1968. It had been years since they won back-to-back pennants, but at least they had good reasons for the slump to fourth place.

The accident that tore up Lonborg's knee caused the difference between twenty-two victories and then only six. Jose Santiago had a sore arm and so did young Ken Brett, who didn't pitch at all for Boston that year. Tony Conigliaro's attempted comeback failed, and George Scott's batting average went from .303 to an anemic .171.

On the plus side was Yastrzemski's third batting title with a surprisingly low .301, but he turned out to be the only American League regular who hit .300. The runner-up was Danny Cater of Oakland, who batted .290. Also Hawk Harrelson's thirty-five home runs and league-leading 109 RBIs helped carry the Red Sox into the first division. Harrelson was voted the American League Player of the Year by *The Sporting News,* which seemed to set well with New England fans. And, if it was any consolation, at least the Red Sox finished ahead of the Yankees. If there was a dominant team from 1968 through 1971, it was the Baltimore Orioles.

Miraculously, Tony Conigliaro's eyesight returned in 1969 and he did come back for a time. On April 8th he hit a two-run homer off Pete Richert of the Orioles, and after the game he told reporters, "It's been a long time between my 104th and 105th home runs. That's as good as I've ever hit a ball."

Tony C.'s return earned for him the Hutch Award, given to

a player who "best exemplified the fighting spirit and burning desire of the late Fred Hutchinson." He continued to hit well in 1970, but recurring eye problems cropped up, and he was traded to California, where he played only half a season. Another comeback try in 1975 proved futile and he was finished for good.

And the Red Sox continued to make trades that nobody—least of all the fans—could quite understand. In early April of 1969 they suddenly traded away their Player of the Year, Ken Harrelson, along with Dick Ellsworth and Juan Pizarro. In return Cleveland sent Sonny Siebert, Vicente Romo and Joe Azcue. Harrelson was stunned and threatened to quit baseball. He didn't, though, and spent three so-so years with the Indians. When he did return to Boston in 1975 it was as color man for telecasts. Joe Azcue, a sub catcher, jumped the team, so Williams had to trade him.

Another deal that caused some soul-searching was the swap with the Yankees that saw the Sox get Danny Cater in exchange for left-handed relief pitcher Sparky Lyle. In all fairness, the Sox were counting on Cater to take over the first-base job left open by the departure of George Scott, while Lyle had had a disappointing 1–7 record the previous season. Evidently the Yankees saw something in Lyle that Boston did not. He became New York's top relief pitcher for six years and won the Cy Young Award in 1977. Cater and a later throw-in, shortstop Mario Guerrero, were completely forgettable.

It was a strike-shortened season in 1972, and was remembered chiefly by Boston fans as another "almost" year, when the Red Sox trailed Detroit by half a game with two games left. Boston lost because Luis Aparicio, an experienced hand at running the bases, twice slipped rounding third base and ended a rally. By then Eddie Kasko was the manager. Dick Williams had departed after the 1969 season.

The Red Sox were also-rans in 1973 and 1974, but better times were on the horizon, and they arrived in 1975 when a dandy pair of rookie outfielders, Fred Lynn and Jim Rice, showed their youthful faces. Together with another youngster, Dwight Evans, they formed one of the finest Red Sox outfields since the days of Speaker, Lewis and Hooper.

Lynn received most of the headlines, and perhaps rightly so. In the month of June, for example, he went on a batting rampage that had the rest of baseball staring wide-eyed. On June 1st, both Lynn and Rice homered to help Luis Tiant—"El Tiante," the roly-poly Latin with the big cigar—eke out a victory over Minnesota, 11-9. Five days later it was Evans who temporarily stole the spotlight with two home runs—one a grand slam—which saved a 13-10 win for Tiant over the same Twins. Next, Tiant beat the Royals, 4-3, all the runs coming on Lynn's three-run shot and Rice's sacrifice fly. On June 18th El Tiante beat the Tigers, 15-1, but nobody even remembered who the pitcher of record was, because Fred Lynn put on a display of power hitting that stunned the Tiger fans at Detroit.

What did Lynn do that was so spectacular? Well, he hit three home runs, one off the roof of the upper deck, the other two into the top deck. He clubbed a triple that missed being another home run by a foot or two. He also banged a single, and a hard line drive that was caught. Net result: five hits for sixteen total bases, ten runs batted in, four runs scored. When the day was done, his average stood at .352, his home-run accumulation was fourteen and his slugging percentage was .640, the best in the league.

Of course, the former USC football player was delighted. He had come to the park early to work on his swing. "It pays to take extra practice," was his comment.

Jim Rice wasn't doing badly either. He had started the season as a DH, but by July 2nd he was installed as the regular left fielder, and celebrated his promotion a few days later by clubbing his sixteenth home run to help El Tiante beat Texas. Unfortunately, in late September, Rice suffered a broken left hand when he was hit by a stray pitch, and was lost for the season. At the time he was batting .309 with twenty-two homers and 102 RBIs. He didn't receive the Rookie of the Year award because the only real choice was Fred Lynn, who became the first major-leaguer ever to win that honor as well as the MVP award.

The Red Sox clinched the pennant on October 7th by beating Oakland, 5-3. That gave them a three-game sweep of the

American League Championship Series. They were back in the World Series competition again, and this time the enemy was the Cincinnati Reds, better known as "the Big Red Machine." The clubs seemed evenly matched and the fans expected an exciting Series. They weren't disappointed.

El Tiante got the opening nod from manager Darrell Johnson, and he was opposed by a stylish young left-hander named Don Gullett. For six innings it was a scoreless duel, with both teams wasting opportunities. In the first inning Evans singled and Yaz walked. With two out Lynn dribbled a grounder to second that Joe Morgan couldn't see because Yaz was running, and Morgan couldn't get to the ball. Evans tried to score but Morgan recovered and fired to Johnny Bench, and that was the third out.

Again in the second the Sox got two runners aboard, this time with nobody out, but Gullett fanned Cecil Cooper and Tiant, then got Evans on a foul fly to right. In the sixth Lynn singled and Petrocelli doubled him to third with only one out. Cooper flied to medium center where Geronimo made an easy catch and threw to Bench, who made a diving tag on Lynn.

The Reds hit the ball solidly in the fifth when Foster opened with a drive off the left-field wall, but fast fielding by Yaz held it to a single. And in the seventh Foster got another hit, but was subsequently thrown out trying to steal. Yaz robbed Dave Concepcion with a diving catch on the wet grass, and that was followed by Ken Griffey's two-base hit. Tiant got out of the inning by walking Concepcion intentionally and getting Gullett out.

It was Tiant who started the seventh-inning carnage by rapping a single to left. Evans bunted, and when Gullett threw the ball away both runners were safe. Second baseman Denny Doyle hit through the left side to load the bases, bringing up Yaz, who hit the first pitch into right field for a single which brought in Tiant.

Clay Carroll relieved Gullett, and he walked Carlton Fisk, forcing in another run. With the left-handed Lynn coming up, Reds manager Sparky Anderson called in Will McEnaney, who got the rookie flash out on strikes. He wasn't as lucky with Petrocelli, whose single to left drove in two more runs.

Rick Burleson's hit brought home the fifth tally, and Cecil Cooper's long drive didn't miss being a home run by much. It was caught, but run number six came in. There was no more scoring by either club. El Tiante lit a big cigar in the clubhouse to celebrate his shutout victory.

There were two surprise starters for the second game, Jack Billingham and Bill Lee. Lee, called "Spaceman" because of his erratic behavior, hadn't started a game since September 19th and hadn't won since August 27th. He had tried five times to win his eighteenth game and wasn't able to do it. Billingham was a veteran, and considering that Gary Nolan, a fifteen-game winner, was available, he didn't seem to be the right choice when the Reds were down by a game.

Billingham got the job done, at least his end of it. He needed some inept baserunning by Cecil Cooper, but mistakes are made even by major-leaguers—or perhaps *especially* by major-leaguers.

Cooper opened the first inning with a hit to left that Foster played into a double. Cooper went to third when Doyle beat out an infield hit, bringing up Yaz. All he could do was hit back to the box, and Billingham pounced on the ball. He wheeled to go to second for the force and possible double play.

There is a basic commandment in baseball that goes like this: With runners on the corners and less than two out, when a ground ball is hit which can be handled by an infielder, the man on third base *must* try to go home. He is, in effect, possibly sacrificing himself in order to stop the double play. If the twin kill is made, at least he tried. If it fails, his team has a run.

Billingham was ready to concede the run because there was nobody out, and he saw a chance to clean the bases. He threw to Concepcion for the force on Doyle. But Cooper hesitated, and Concepcion saw it. The Reds shortstop made the force and threw home to the thundering Cooper at the plate. Yaz, meanwhile, had alertly gone to second on the play, and he came in on Fisk's single.

Joe Morgan gave Cooper an object lesson in baserunning in the fourth inning when the same situation arose for the Reds.

With one out he walked and took third on a Johnny Bench single. When Perez grounded into a force at second, Morgan did not wait, but promptly lit out for home and scored. It was a tied-up ball game.

In the sixth the Sox regained the lead on a single by Yaz, an error by Concepcion and a two-out ground single up the middle by Petrocelli. The Red Sox entered the ninth inning holding a 2–1 lead, and Bill Lee was in top form. All he needed was three outs and the Sox would be two games up on the Reds. He didn't make it.

Johnny Bench came up and drilled Lee's pitch to right for two bases. Johnson wasted no time and promptly replaced Lee, who came off the mound to a standing ovation. Lee was succeeded by Dick Drago. And Drago forced Perez to hit a gound ball to second base for the out. Perez too was showing how to execute the fundamentals of baseball, by following this dictum: With a runner on second and nobody out, hit the ball to the right side so that the runner can go to third, from which point he can score on a long fly, a wild pitch, a passed ball or a deep grounder. Bench hustled to third.

It seemed that the strategy would fail when Foster lifted a fly to short left. Wet weather or not, this was not the time to find out if Yaz still knew how to make the throw to the plate. Bench stayed put. The Reds, trailing 2–1, were down to their last out. Dave Concepcion, whose error had led to Boston's second run, was the next batter.

Concepcion bounced one back through the middle. Doyle grabbed the ball with an acrobatic backhand stab, but he had no play anywhere. Concepcion was safe and Bench tied the game.

With Ken Griffey at the plate and the game tied, Concepcion took off for second and slid in under Burleson's tag. Again the Red Sox were guilty of loose play. Even Concepcion said as much.

"I missed the bag," he confessed after the game. "But Burleson maybe didn't see it, or else he just didn't return for the tag." Regardless of the reason, Concepcion was in scoring position. Griffey hammered a double to left center and Concepcion sprinted home with what proved to be the winning run. Rawly Eastwick, the Reds' prize rookie relief specialist, turned the Sox away in the home half and the Reds had the game, 3–2.

"We're lucky to get out of here with our lives," said Sparky Anderson with a sigh.

The Reds won the third game in ten innings, 6–5, but the score and outcome took second place to one of the most bizarre plays ever seen in a World Series. It can be said that an umpire's decision won the game for Cincinnati.

Sure, it's important that six home runs were hit, three by each team. It is also exciting to learn that a two-run drive by Evans in the ninth inning tied the score and sent the game into overtime. What happened in the tenth inning was the nub of the contest.

With Geronimo on base and nobody out, Sparky Anderson sent a sub named Ed Armbrister to the plate with instructions to lay down a bunt. Dutifully, Armbrister squared away and dropped the ball in front of the plate. Armbrister started out of the batter's box just as Fisk came out from behind the plate to grab the ball. It looked very much as if he had a chance for a second-to-first double play. Somehow, Fisk and Armbrister found themselves falling all over each other, and when they had untangled, Fisk fired the ball over second and into center field. Geronimo went to third and Armbrister took second. The Red Sox came swarming out of the dugout screaming about interference, but plate umpire Barnett refused to allow it.

Left-hander Roger Moret came in to strike out pinch hitter Merve Rettenmund. Then he walked Pete Rose intentionally to load the bases. Joe Morgan ended the game by driving the ball over the head of Fred Lynn, who was playing in because a long fly would have ended the game anyway.

After the game was over, Barnett emerged from the dressing room to explain his ruling on the play. He said, "It was not interference, it was a collision. For an interference call there has to be an attempt to impede the catcher on the part of the hitter. I saw it as a collision. It was a judgment play and that's how I called it."

Not to worry—at least for the time being. El Tiante put

down his cigar, strode to the mound for game four, and the next time he lit up the Series was tied at two games each. The Reds scored two runs in the first and two more in the fourth. The Red Sox scored all five of their runs in a fourth-inning outburst. Cincinnati pitcher Fred Norman got through three innings before the roof fell in on him. He and Pedro Borbon absorbed all the punishment.

The parade of runs began when Fisk and Lynn singled and Norman wild-pitched them along. Evans tripled, Burleson hustled a single into a double, Tiant singled, Tony Perez messed up a grounder and Yastrzemski singled. That took care of Boston's requirements. Tiant permitted the Reds to come within a run, but when the Reds started to threaten, Luis would go into that stuttering stretch position that was so hard to figure out. It was Boston, 5–4.

Game five started out as a battle of left-handers, Reggie Cleveland for Boston and Don Gullett for Cincinnati. The Reds won it, 6–2, because the silent bat of Tony Perez finally came to life.

The Red Sox got on the scoreboard in the first inning, only to have Perez, the thirty-three-year-old RBI specialist from Cuba, nail one over the fence in left center, a four-hundred-foot smash. The Reds edged ahead in the fifth on Gullett's single and a long opposite-field fly by Rose that dropped inches fair in left field. Juan Beniquez, playing left field because Yaz was doing the honors at first base, ran the ball down and had a chance to get Gullett, who was racing for the plate, but his throw went over everybody's head and Gullett was in.

In the sixth it was all over. Morgan walked, and that was a mistake because he proceeded to drive Cleveland crazy with his long leads. The Sox pitcher kept throwing to first and Morgan kept diving back to the bag. Cleveland threw seven times to first, then a strike to Johnny Bench. Then he threw four more times to first before delivering another pitch that Bench fouled off. Another five throws made the total sixteen to first base and just two to the plate. Their little game ended when Bench singled to right, sending Morgan to third. Bench took second on the vain throw to catch Morgan.

Up stepped Perez, who slugged a 2-and-1 pitch over the left-field fence for his second home run of the game.

Gullett pitched eight and two thirds innings and went out of the game with a 6–2 advantage. Eastwick got the final out and now the Reds led, three games to two.

The sixth game, played at Fenway, had to be one of the most thrilling ever played in any Series. The high points came thick and fast during the twelve-inning, four-hour-and-one-minute marathon, and there was so much to see and so much to talk about later that a run-by-run account would be an exercise in futility. Better to cite the electrifying moments that brought the crowd to its feet again and again and again.

It all began in the first inning when Fred Lynn, the sweetheart of all Boston, clouted a three-run homer to give Boston the lead. Cincinnati fought back with three runs in the fifth, two in the seventh and one in the eighth to take a 6–3 lead. El Tiante didn't have it that night. He went seven-plus innings, gave up all the Cincinnati runs on eleven hits and was replaced by Roger Moret.

With hope fading in the bottom of the eighth, the little-used Bernie Carbo saw to it that all was right with the world by pinch hitting a three-run homer to even the score. Then the Sox loaded the bases in the bottom of the ninth with nobody out, and Fred Lynn came to the plate. Pandemonium, that's what it was, like a thousand cannons going off at once. The groans were just as load when Lynn hit a windblown fly to George Foster in left that didn't travel more than 180 feet. As Foster made the grab, Denny Doyle foolishly tried to score the winning run and was cut down by Foster's strong throw to Bench.

With one out in the eleventh, Joe Morgan rammed a sure home run toward the right-field seats. Dwight Evans committed bare-faced robbery when he plucked the ball right out of the seats. Only six innings previously, Fred Lynn had leaped against the wall trying to grab a ball that was out of reach, crashed into the wall and lay still for a horrifying moment. Lynn stayed in the game despite an aching back.

In the twelfth it was over. Sparky Anderson had used eight pitchers during the game, none of them pitching to more than nine batters. The last one was Pat Darcy. He grooved one to Carlton Fisk and the big catcher hit a smash into the air.

For an instant he stood at the plate as the ball soared out

toward left field. It was long enough, but was it fair or foul? Fisk began to twitch, using body English to coax the ball fair. And it was fair, hitting the neon pole at the corner of the screen. Fisk leaped high and circled the bases clapping his hands. When he reached the plate he landed on it with both feet as the Fenway Park faithful went berserk.

Afterward, Pete Rose—good old Charley Hustle—seemed to be in good spirits. "I really enjoyed the game," he said after it was over. Mulling over Evans's grab of Morgan's shot, he said approvingly, "God, that Evans is a bitch. He doesn't make catches like that all the time, does he?" Then he added, "What a game! If this isn't the national pastime . . . well, it's the best advertisement you could have for baseball."

Joe Morgan was a lot more affirmative in his outlook. In the locker room he said to a reporter, "Look around. You don't see anyone hanging his head here, do you? It's not the end of the world. We've lost games like this before and we've bounced back. And we'll do it again, just wait and see."

Morgan's words were prophetic. Just as the details of the sixth game were too joyous for Red Sox fans to bother with, so were the itemized lists of game seven too agonizing for the fans to bear. The Reds won the World Series with a come-from-behind effort, 4–3. Yet, to a great extent, those details prevented the Red Sox from winning the Championship of baseball.

In Boston's first inning, Bernie Carbo opened with a double. Doyle tried to hit to right in approved fashion, and he did, except that it was a short fly, not a grounder, and Carbo couldn't advance to third. One run was lost right there.

Another key play was in the sixth after the Red Sox had built a 3–0 lead. With a man on first, Rose sent a double-play grounder which could have ended the inning. Doyle hurried the relay and the ball sailed over Yaz's head. Instead of the inning being over, Tony Perez came to bat and lined a home run to put the Reds back in the game.

In the eighth Evans opened with a walk and Burleson couldn't lay down a bunt in two tries. With an 0-and-2 count he swung away and grounded into a short-second-to-first double play.

And how did the Reds win the game in the ninth? On a walk, a sacrifice and Joe Morgan's bloop pop fly that fell in just behind second base. In the final analysis, the Reds could execute properly in the clutch, the Red Sox couldn't.

Boston made a bold move to buy a pennant in 1976 and the mortally ill Tom Yawkey showed he hadn't put his wallet away in mothballs. Charles O. Finley, the irascible owner of the Oakland Athletics, had been losing a great deal of money, and he was stuck with three stars who would shortly be lost in the free-agent market because Finley couldn't—and wouldn't—pay those inflated salaries the players were demanding. In June he unloaded his top three: Vida Blue, an outstanding left-handed pitcher, to the Yankees for a cash purchase price of $1.5 million. The Red Sox paid one million dollars each for ace relief pitcher Rollie Fingers and outfielder Joe Rudi. It looked like Finley was solvent again and both the Yanks and Red Sox had some valuable additions.

Three days later commissioner Bowie Kuhn voided both transactions and sent the players back to Oakland. His reason: "The sales are not in the best interests of baseball."

To Finley, the Yankees and the Red Sox, such reasoning made absolutely no sense whatsoever. Finley promptly filed a ten-million-dollar suit against Kuhn (he eventually lost it). Darrell Johnson snarled, "I can't understand what went through Kuhn's head. What's the difference between these deals and maybe selling Joe Lahoud to Texas for $25,000? What's the dividing line?"

On July 9th, 1976, Tom Yawkey, aged seventy-three, died of leukemia. Many insiders knew how sick he was, but somehow it seemed impossible to think of the Boston Red Sox without Tom Yawkey after almost forty-four years. He did not live to see his beloved team win a World Series.

Tributes came from everywhere, one of the most moving from Sparky Anderson. "Tom Yawkey was the greatest gentleman I've ever met in baseball," Anderson said quietly. "Eddie Kasko introduced me to him the day we got to Boston for the World Series. He took me upstairs to Yawkey's office, and there he was, wearing an old, moth-eaten Red Sox jacket. I said to myself, 'This is a multimillionaire?'

"After we won, during the clubhouse celebration, I got word there was a call for me. It was Tom Yawkey, on the line to congratulate me. The man was all class."

But life went on. On May 13th, 1978, the American League approved the sale of the Red Sox to a group headed by Mrs. Jean Yawkey, former Red Sox reserve catcher Haywood Sullivan and team trainer Buddy LeRoux for a reported price of fifteen million dollars. Jean Yawkey, Tom's widow, became the club president. Sullivan, once a substitute catcher with the Red Sox and since 1965 vice-president for player personnel, would head up the baseball operation. LeRoux, who had been the team's trainer from 1966 to 1974, would handle the business and administrative end of the Red Sox.

In late March, as the Red Sox began their trek north for the preseason final exhibition games, the club worked out a trade with the Cleveland Indians that was to prove one of the finest deals in recent Sox history. Pitchers Rick Wise, Mike Paxton, catcher Bo Diaz and outfielder Ted Cox went to the Indians for pitcher Dennis Eckersley and catcher Fred Kendall. Eckersley did everything the Red Sox management expected of him and then some, as he once again regained the form he displayed in 1972 when he was named Rookie of the Year. He rang up victory after victory over the best teams in the league. He became the Red Sox "stopper," the ace of the mound corps, and finished the season with a fine 20–12 record.

Nineteen seventy-eight was also the year that will sicken the heart of Fenway partisans even after the angel Gabriel comes to Earth and blows a tune on his trumpet. It wasn't merely that Boston lost another playoff and lost the pennant, but mostly that the Yankees took the flag and beat Boston in a showdown game.

It had been a tough season for both teams. On July 19th, the Yankees seemed out of it, trailing Boston by fourteen games. Don Zimmer was at the helm for Boston. Darrell Johnson, who had been voted Manager of the Year in 1975, was dismissed in mid-July of 1976; Zimmer, a Red Sox coach, replaced him.

Suddenly the Yankees made their move upward while the Red Sox went into a slump. The Yanks, in one of baseball's most remarkable comebacks, won fifty-two of seventy-three to catch the Sox and actually go ahead by three and a half games. Boston's slide was marked by fourteen losses in seventeen games from August 30th to September 16th, but in a sudden reversal of form the Sox surged ahead to win eleven of the last thirteen, the final seven in a row, enabling them to tie the Yanks on the final day of the season. It was again time for a sudden-death playoff.

Mike Torrez took the mound for Boston, the same Mike Torrez who had been Yankee property until he became a free agent at the end of 1977 and was signed up to a seven-year, $2.5-million-dollar contract by Boston. His opponent was a slim young southpaw named Ron Guidry, who had an overpowering fastball and a slider that dropped down like a cyclone. Guidry, who would post a stunning 25–3 record with a 1.75 ERA, earned the nickname "Louisiana Lightnin'," and not without reason.

Through the first six innings Torrez shut out the Yanks, keeping them at bay with just two hits. He was magnificent, and he had a two-run lead after Yaz hit his seventeenth home run in the second frame and Jim Rice scored Burleson in the sixth with a base hit.

In the seventh Torrez fell apart. Chris Chambliss and Roy White singled. Up came Bucky Dent, whose season average was .243, including four home runs. Dent fouled a pitch off his foot and spent some time walking around to shake off the pain. Mickey Rivers had a short conversation with Dent and persuaded him to use a Mickey Rivers model bat.

Torrez came over with a fastball that was up and in. Dent went after it and lifted a high fly to left field that just seemed to carry and carry and carry . . . until it went into the screen for a three-run homer. Just like that the game turned around and the Yankees had the lead. The fans were stunned. Torrez was stunned. Even Bucky Dent was stunned. But he shook off his surprise long enough to circle the bases.

The Yanks weren't through yet. Paul Blair got a two-bagger and catcher Thurman Munson doubled him home to make the score 4–2. An inning later Reggie Jackson clouted a home run to make it 5–2.

The Red Sox came back battling all the way. In the eighth inning Jerry Remy doubled, Yaz singled him home, and Fred Lynn saw to it that Yaz scored, to make the count 5-4 going into the ninth.

Again the Red Sox rallied as they had done in the previous inning. Along the way Yankee right fielder Lou Piniella contributed two outstanding plays, fighting through the glare of the sun to prevent more runs from scoring. Though ace reliever Goose Gossage was throwing darts, the Red Sox got Rick Burleson to third base and Jerry Remy to first with two men out. Carl Yastrzemski was the batter as the crowd begged him to come through with a hit.

Sad but true, Yaz suffered almost the same fate as the mighty Casey. With a 1-and-0 count, the Goose sent his best fastball, a rising pitch that Yaz swung at. He got under the pitch and popped it foul just outside third, where a grateful Graig Nettles squeezed it for the final out.

"It's a shame this wasn't a seven-game series and it wasn't the World Series," Yankee owner George Steinbrenner told the Boston players. "We are the two best teams in baseball. We won, but you didn't lose."

Reggie Jackson went through the Boston roster shaking hands. "Both of us should be champions," he said sincerely.

Carl Yastrzemski agreed. "We have everything in the world to be proud of. The only thing we don't have is the ring." Then he added, "The Red Sox versus the Yankees is the greatest rivalry in sports."

It was the year Jim Rice came into his own. He was named Most Valuable Player in the American League, defeating Ron Guidry by 352 to 291 points. Magnanimously, Rice suggested that the reason he won was due to the fact that he played in all 163 games, while Guidry pitched in standard rotation. Rice's stats were awesome. He led both leagues in such departments as hits (213), home runs (46), RBIs (139), triples (15) and slugging percentage (.600). There was also nothing wrong with his .315 batting average and 121 runs scored.

The Red Sox were fully aware of Rice's accomplishments. The front office also knew that he would become a free agent after 1980 and they acted accordingly. Rice became another of baseball's instant millionaires, inking a seven-year contract that was rumored to amount to $5.4 million.

As for Guidry, he won the AL Cy Young Award. Oddly, he was named *Major League* Player of the Year by *The Sporting News*. Rice had to be content with the newspaper's *American League* Player of the Year designation.

Chapter XIII

IN 1977 the Red Sox signed Mike Torrez away from the Yankees in the free-agent market. In 1978 Yankee owner George Steinbrenner returned the favor by signing a Red Sox pet, Luis Tiant, to a New York contract. It was a multipurpose pact calling for a total of $875,000, which included two years as a player and the next ten years as Steinbrenner's scout in Latin American countries.

In some ways it was surprising to see the Red Sox let El Tiante move to New York, yet in other aspects it wasn't too hard to understand. For openers, there was Luis's age to consider. He claimed to be thirty-eight years old, but wiser heads insisted he was somewhat older, although no one said how much older. Perhaps that helped explain why no other team went after him in the free-agent merry-go-round. Except for a few hardy souls, most players in Tiant's age category had stopped active duty years ago.

Also, Tiant obviously wasn't the pitcher he had been. He had come to the Red Sox during the 1971 season after having been released by the Twins and Braves. It seemed a bitter end to a career which started in Cuba and Mexico, then began to grow with the Cleveland Indians, climaxing with a twenty-one-victory year in 1968.

In 1969 Tiant's career seemed to shift into reverse. There were hassles with manager Alvin Dark and the Indians' lack of hitting and defense to contend with. Also, the Cleveland sportswriters were a good deal less than kind—or accurate, for that matter.

On May 15th Tiant was 0–7 and growing more frustrated daily. Later in the month Dark used him as a mop-up man against Seattle when the game was hopelessly out of reach. This gave rise to the printed rumor that Tiant was being taken out of the starting rotation. One snide Cleveland sportswriter called Tiant "the highest paid relief pitcher in baseball."

Tiant was ripping mad, and so was Dark. The two men might have had their differences, but the story just wasn't true, since Dark had no intention of using Tiant as a fireman. That single relief appearance was all Dark had planned for him. Tiant certainly was in the rotation, and he proved his right to be there by winning seven of his next eight starts, the lone loss being a 4–3 decision to Chicago. One victory was a two-hit shutout against California, another was a ten-strikeout job against the Yankees.

Again the fates began to taunt Tiant. He lost ten of his next eleven decisions. In three games the Indians scored one run for him. In three others the Indians were shut out. Luis finished the year with a 9–20 record. The next season he was in Minnesota.

With the Twins Tiant reeled off six straight wins, but he was pitching with constant pain. He was trying to throw hard but the ball was traveling slow, and the pangs in his shoulder were driving him up the wall. The situation came to a head when Tiant felt a distinct pop and a sharp stab of pain in the shoulder. Three days later El Tiante could scarcely hold a baseball, let alone throw it.

X-rays revealed the source of the trouble, a fractured scapula, which is the wing bone behind the shoulder. The only cure the medics could suggest was rest. Tiant was placed on the twenty-one-day disabled list and the Twins called up a rookie named Bert Blyleven to take his place on the roster.

Tiant didn't return to active duty until the beginning of August, and while the injury had healed and the pain was gone, the problem now was mental. He was actually afraid to go all out and cut loose. Tiant was 1–3 in 1970.

For the Twins' purposes, Tiant was finished. The team had no use for a pitcher whose arm seemed to have gone dead, and he was given his unconditional release. Through the assistance of an old Dodger pitcher named Ed Roebuck, Tiant got a thirty-day conditional contract from the Atlanta Braves and was told to report to their affiliate in Richmond, Virginia.

For no apparent reason—except that perhaps it was again mental—Tiant's fastball returned. Richmond manager Clyde King watched Tiant go five innings against Bradenton and shook his head, puzzled.

"Why did the Minnesota people let you go?" King asked.

"I don't know," Tiant shrugged.

A Pittsburgh scout asked, "What's wrong with your arm?"

"Nothing," answered Tiant. "All I need is work."

Tiant couldn't get in much work because of rainouts and other postponements. Meanwhile, stories of his returned fastball reached the ears of Lee Stange, the Red Sox minor-league pitching coach. Tiant's minor league statistics seemed to belie his renewed ability to pitch in the big leagues. He was 1–3—in the *minors*—with a 6.26 ERA. He had allowed twenty-two hits, seventeen walks and sixteen runs in twenty-three innings. That was big-league stuff? Yet Stange could not disbelieve what he had heard. He consulted Red Sox officials and was told to find out when Tiant's thirty-day option was up. When the date arrived Clyde King wanted the Braves to call him up. Tiant, he thought, could be ready once his timing returned and he got the work he needed. Atlanta refused and Tiant was a free man.

The Red Sox gave Tiant a full contract to pitch for Louisville. The cigar-smoking Cuban didn't disappoint. He was 2–2 with the Colonels, with a 2.61 ERA, twenty-nine strikeouts and eleven walks in thirty-one innings.

"My control still isn't right," he apologized.

The Red Sox thought his control was good enough. Just twenty days after he joined the Colonels, Tiant was on his way to take his turn with the parent club.

Tiant started six times in July, winning none and losing four. In one start he went seven innings against the Yankees, losing 2–1 on Roy White's home run. In another start Luis pitched ten shutout innings, but he was taken out for a pinch hitter and received no credit one way or the other. Whether through lack of work or a bad streak he was tiring in the late innings. Kasko put him in the bullpen and Tiant pitched pretty good ball, but he was 0–6 until August 31st when he finally got his first victory in more than a year.

Luis rounded into shape soon enough and became one of the league's best. He won twenty games in 1973, twenty-two in 1974, twenty-one in 1976. He was just as valuable in the clubhouse or in the dugout, needling the Sox or their opponents with his own brand of humor. "Loo-ie! Loo-ie!" The fans would take up the chant whenever he strutted onto the field, whether to pitch or just to be seen. Then, by Boston standards, he began to slip, going 12–8 in 1977 and 13–8 in 1978. Age was creeping up on the portly *señor* and when his contract ran out he was offered another for just one year. He turned it down. The Red Sox bid him farewell and allowed him to find his own way in the free-agent derby.

"After all I did for them, it wasn't fair," mourned El Tiante. And he had a point. Since coming up to the Hub he had won 122 and lost eighty-one, being one of only three pitchers in the history of the Red Sox to win twenty or more three times, and the first to win that many since Jim Lonborg back in 1967.

With the Yankees Tiant enjoyed one pretty fair season and one ordinary season. Then Steinbrenner also let him go.

With or without Tiant the Red Sox had good teams. They just didn't win the pennant. In 1977 the club won ninety-seven games, the most since 1946, but they ended the season tied with Baltimore for second place. Pitching was the problem, as it had been off and on for years. That year no starter won more than twelve games; high man was Bill Campbell, a big righthander with a baffling screwball who won thirteen and saved thirty-one in relief. An injury to Fred Lynn's ankle didn't help matters either. In his first two seasons Lynn hit .331 and .314, but hobbling around on a gimpy foot, all he could do was .260 in 1977.

The Red Sox rebuilt. They got Mike Torrez and Dennis Eckersley for the starting rotation and added Dick Drago and Tom Bergmeier to the bullpen, plus Jerry Remy at second base, but the net result was that playoff game in 1978. Perhaps a healthy Bill Campbell might have helped. After his big season, Campbell pitched only 106 innings over the next two years, going 10–9, with a total of thirteen saves. Butch Hobson had the miseries too, trying to play with a bump on his elbow the size of a golf ball.

In 1979, injuries to Fisk and Remy took the heart out of the team. Fisk was a complete mystery at first. He had played with cracked ribs during the stretch run the previous season, then suddenly he couldn't throw to second and catch a runner even if his grandmother were trying to steal on him. A few doctors probed and poked but they couldn't find anything wrong. Finally, the club physician, Dr. Arthur Pappas, saw what was bothering Fisk. A tiny bit of bone had broken off and was lodged in the elbow joint. X-rays taken during spring training the following year showed that the fragment had been absorbed.

The injury to Remy was more obvious. All coaches tell base runners never to do anything halfway, never to hesitate, always to play affirmatively. Remy evidently forgot that. On June 30th, in a game against the Yankees, Remy started to slide, hesitated, slid anyway and caught his foot. He felt something pop in his knee and had to be carried off the field. He rested until August, tried to come back, and had his knee buckle when he tried to run to first base. Remy had been batting .304 before the injury.

In 1980 the Red Sox were a complete mystery team. Over the first third of the season they had trouble staying close to the .500 mark, and there were all sorts of valid reasons. There were some slumps at the wrong times. Lynn, for instance, went 1-for-24 during one stretch, but broke out with 13-for-18 when his stroke returned. Rice struggled through 1-for-35, then came back with 8-for-23.

And the injuries came in clusters. At one point the Red Sox lost five players in five consecutive games. First, pitcher Chuck Rainey strained a muscle when he threw a curveball, and had to go on the twenty-one-day disabled list. Then Baltimore's Al Bumbry lined a pitch off reliever Skip Lockwood's rib cage. Next, Yastrzemski made a diving stab at a fly ball, injured his back and went to the hospital for a spell. After that, Tom Burgmeier, the workhorse of the bullpen, developed a soreness in his pitching shoulder and he was sidelined. Finally, in the first game after the All-Star break, Jerry Remy tore up his left knee again and was sent home on crutches.

Another reason for the Red Sox failure of 1980 was the team's puzzling inability to win at Fenway. A look at their record just prior to the All-Star break, when they trailed the Yankees by nine and a half games, told it all: 25–16 in other parks, 16–20 at home.

Along the way, during those also-ran years, the Red Sox learned that the free-agent market was not necessarily the best way to stock a team's roster. Maybe George Steinbrenner knew the secret, but not Yawkey, nor Sullivan either. The Red Sox' efforts met with mixed success. Mike Torrez, who had signed a fat contract, was certainly no world-beater. Skip Lockwood, a $400,000 relief pitcher who had previously toiled for the New York Mets, developed soreness in his arm and was no help. Tony Perez, on the other hand, was a nifty pickup. After the loss of Bob Watson, the Red Sox shopped around for a replacement at first base and came upon Tony Perez, a thirty-eight-year-old baseball slugger who had been a seven-time All-Star with Cincinnati's Big Red Machine, then switched to Montreal. Perez, Don Zimmer found to his delight, was like a mechanical man—just wind him up and he bats in a run. Tony slugged twenty-five home runs for the Sox and drove in 105 runs.

Basically, it was a bad starting rotation and the unending rash of injuries that felled the Red Sox. Jim Rice, hit on the wrist by a pitched ball, was out for twenty-six games, Yaz, because of a fractured rib, was inactive the final month of the campaign. Still, a third-place finish was not exactly what the front office or the fans had in mind. Everyone knew there would be a flock of new faces in the area pretty soon, but nobody could have predicted that so many of the old favorites would be gone.

It started in the traditional way with the firing of the manager. Listing the reasons for Zimmer's dismissal, general manager Haywood Sullivan said bluntly, "We decided to make a change because of economics, fan reaction, public relations and change for change's sake." Sullivan conceded that Zimmer had done everything humanly possible under the circumstances, that he was a manager with fine baseball sense. What had finally undone the Red Sox was the poor performances of the team's three top starters, Mike Torrez, Dennis Eckersley and Bob Stanley, who had a combined record of 31–36. Teams do not win with that kind of pitching. Torrez was the big disappointment. In his three years with the Red Sox, big Mike had gone 41–40, hardly the kind of numbers expected from an expensive top-line pitcher.

Zimmer, whose Red Sox teams had won 411 and lost 315, had to fight back the tears as he sat beside Sullivan during the press conference. "I'd like the people of New England to think I'm a good man," said the gutsy, roly-poly man. Then he hurried from the room. He was snapped up by Texas.

The so-called "option year" also gave the Red Sox a huge headache. After 1980, both Rick Burleson and Fred Lynn had one year left on their contracts. Lynn was hinting about a multiyear contract at about a million per year, and Burleson about a third less than that, and perhaps that was partly what Sullivan was alluding to when he mentioned "economics" at the press conference.

Sullivan was so convinced that he would be unable to sign his stars that he went to the winter meetings looking to trade them. As he put it when asked about the possibility of retaining them, "It's about forty to sixty," Yet he was optimistic about a trade or two. Although they were demanding plenty of money, they were quality players, very marketable, and even if they went through the free-agent market the following year a club would have to open the bank vault to get them. Sullivan was willing to let another club owner deal with that problem. He wanted to get what he could in a swap for his talented shortstop and center fielder.

The Burleson trade was easy enough. He went to the California Angels (Butch Hobson soon joined him there) in exchange for a third baseman named Carney Lansford, an excellent relief pitcher in Mark Clear, and outfielder Rick Miller, who had worn a Boston uniform before.

The cases of Lynn and Carlton Fisk were completely different. Fisk had also expressed dissatisfaction economically, but indicated that he would prefer to stay in Boston. Somehow the Boston front office lost track of the date and mailed out Lynn's and Fisk's contracts a day or so late, so that technically they could become free agents. Hurriedly, Sullivan dispatched

Lynn to California for pitcher Frank Tanana and outfielder Joe Rudi. Somebody up there was probably chuckling over the arrival of Rudi in Boston. Several years earlier Boston had tried to buy him from Charles O. Finley for a million dollars, only to have commissioner Bowie Kuhn negate the deal.

The Fisk affair was a total loss to the Red Sox. Rather than sign a Boston contract he went through the free-agent draft and signed to play with the Chicago White Sox.

As a replacement for Zimmer, the Red Sox lured Ralph Houk out of retirement. Houk, a rugged Marine combat officer in World War II, had broken into baseball with the Yankee organization as a catcher, but during his playing days he was practically invisible. In his eight active years he played a total of ninety-one games, forty-one of them as a rookie in 1947, but his career never got off the ground because the Yankees were breaking in another young man named Yogi Berra, and shortly thereafter along came a gentleman named Elston Howard, the latter also serving the Red Sox in the twilight of a great career.

Houk became the Yankees' manager in 1961 and ran off three pennants in a row. He was also, for a while, vice-president and general manager of the club. After serving New York for eleven years he went to Detroit, where he managed for five years with indifferent results. Only in 1978, his final year at the helm of the Tigers, did he have a winning season. Then he retired in 1978 to do some fishin' and whittlin' at home in Pompano Beach, Florida. The inactivity got to him, the Red Sox called him and he jumped at the opportunity to get back in action.

Judging strictly on the basis of past performances, Houk knew he would have enough hitting to get by. What he needed was pitching, and he embarked upon two reclamation jobs, Mike Torrez and Bill Campbell. Houk also had hopes that Dennis Eckersley, who had shown sporadic signs of coming around since his injury in mid-1979, would regain his confidence and effectiveness.

Torrez, Houk saw, had been going to his breaking stuff too often, which was probably one of the reasons he ran out of gas in the late innings. Torrez was instructed to concentrate on throwing nothing but his fastball, which tended to stretch and strengthen the muscles of what was essentially a strong arm. Campbell, who had pitched in pain for so long, had been throwing with more velocity in spring training. Houk's practiced eye could see improvement on the horizon, but it would take time and patience. After having suffered through the decline and fall of the once proud Yankees through most of the 1960s, Houk had developed Job's attitude. He refused to rush Campbell along.

Then came the great baseball strike of 1981, and approximately one third of the season was spent in endless talk and negotiations by the club owners and the players' union. The big issue was compensation for the loss of a free agent from the team that acquired the player, and all sorts of proposals were thrown on the table, examined and rejected. It would be pointless to name a winner, but the loser was obvious: the baseball fan. Baseball had been and always would be "the summer game" for the American sports enthusiast. In August, baseball resumed, with the split season that left everybody puzzled.

The Yankees were declared winners of the first half of the season, with the Orioles, Brewers, Detroit and the Red Sox finishing in that order. The Bosox finished in fifth place, four games below the leading Yanks. In the Western Division, Billy Martin's Oakland club copped the first-place half of the race and so the Yankees and Oakland automatically moved into the final playoffs.

The Red Sox got off swiftly after the strike was finally settled in August, and due to some excellent pitching by Eckersley and rookie Bob Ojeda the Sox surprised their cohorts by hanging close to the Yankees and the Tigers. On September 19th the Red Sox tallied seven runs in the eighth inning to beat the Yankees at Fenway and move to within one and a half games of first place. The next day the Sox again had an easy time beating the Yankees, 4–1, to move within half a game of the leading New Yorkers. It was the pitching of Bruce Hurst and Bill Campbell and the timely hitting of Tony Perez, who drove out two home runs, that beat the Yanks. A week later, Ojeda, a twenty-three-year-old rookie, came within one inning of a no-hit game against the Yankees. It was the finest pitching performance by a Red Sox hurler in recent years. Ojeda held the Yanks hitless until Cerone led off the ninth inning with a pinch-hit line double. Winfield doubled and the Yanks had their first and only run. Mark Clear relieved Ojeda and preserved a 2–1 win for the Sox.

The Red Sox continued to battle the league leaders right until the last week of the season. They went down to the final few days of the season before a 10–5 wipeout by Milwaukee ended all playoff hopes for the Sox. Houk and the fans, however, had seen the promise of better days to come.

Carney Lansford became the new darling of Boston. He slugged the ball all through the season and led the American League with a great .339 batting average. Pitcher Mark Clear came through with an 8–3 season, nine saves and eighty-two strikeouts. Rick Miller and Tony Perez were outstanding, and rookie Rich Gedman, a twenty-one-year-old from Worcester, surprised Houk with his fine work behind the plate and his sturdy hitting.

The reclamation projects didn't turn out badly. Torrez was 10–3, a vast improvement over the previous year. Bob Stanley was 10–8. Bill Campbell began to pitch well. He was 1–1 with seven saves. Some of the expected hitting wasn't up to par, including .284 by Jim Rice, and Yaz's .246, but there were compensations in .307 by Remy and .296 by Dwight Evans.

All in all the Burleson-Hobson trade turned out to be the surprise of the year, as Lansford, Clear and Miller played outstanding ball. Houk didn't really expect much from Tanana and Rudi. Both men were injured and were slow in responding. But the future never looked better, according to Houk.

There are, to be sure, any number of question marks about the Red Sox, some of them to be answered in a year, perhaps two. Yastrzemski will play again in 1982, but Carl can't go on forever, and the day must come when he'll put away the spikes for good. Even the most hopeful fans know that the Sox will always have pitching problems. They always have had. Perhaps next year, or the next, the promising sore-armed hurlers will come back and the likes of Bob Stanley, Frank Tanana, Dennis Eckersley, Mike Torrez and Tom Burgmeier will join Mark Clear, Bob Ojeda, Jerry King and Chuck Rainey to give the Sox one of the best pitching staffs in the league.

And, said manager Houk, "A healthy Yaz, Perez, Joe Rudi,

Jim Rice and Dwight Evans, another great year by Lansford, and we'll be in the thick of the championship for the next couple of years."

There has been a glorious past for the Red Sox, some cruel intervening years and a satisfying present, but the greatest Red Sox years under the skillful guidance of Haywood Sullivan and Ralph Houk are still ahead for the colorful team from the Land of the Bean and the Cod. . . .

About the Author

HOWARD LISS was born in Brooklyn, New York, but has been a rabid Boston Red Sox follower, and writer for more than 25 years. It was an interview with the great Sox slugger, Ted Williams, that prompted Liss to become a Red Sox rooter. Along with his famous Boston born colleague, author Robin Moore, Liss has covered some 85 Red Sox games each season, during the past 15 years. One of the most prolific sportswriters in America, Liss is the author of more than 60 sports books, including biographies of Willie Mays, Yogi Berra, and many others. Currently, Liss is busy writing the Ted Williams biography.